SLOT MACHINE STRATEGY

SLOT MACHINE STRATEGY

Winning Methods for Hitting the Jackpot

MacIntyre Symms

The Lyons Press
Guilford, Connecticut
An imprint of The Globe Pequot Press

CONTENTS

ACKNOWLEDGMENTS

The author wishes to thank the following people: Edward C. Behringer; Michael Benson; Rita Benson; Annie Darrigan; Jake Elwell; Scott Frommer; Enrica Gadler; Tony and Marie Grasso; Curt Kentner; Eric Ketchum; Paul McCaffrey; Greig O'Brien; and Bert Randolph Sugar.

SLOT MACHINE STRATEGY

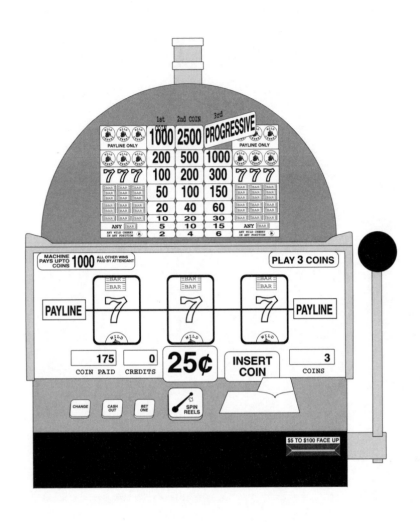

INTRODUCTION
THE PULSE OF THE CASINO

For me and the slot machine, it was love at first sight—and sound. Actually, it was the sound that got me first. In fact, it's the first thing you notice when you enter a casino: the cacophonic tintinnabulation of the slot machines.

Like jukeboxes of chance, slot machines are ringing and dinging and gonging and humming 24 hours a day, seven days a week. The sound of thousands of slot machines all operating simultaneously is the life-beat of a gambling establishment.

That is the sound that gives casinos their pulse.

Well, even if I first fell in love with the sound of slot machines, the first sight pushed me right over the edge into la-la land, ga-ga in love. I searched out the source of that sound and, ahhh—there they were.

1

Row after row of them, back to back, shiny, many of them art deco in design, their whirling reels emitting a light show, rippling with rainbow color. At the time it seemed very psychedelic. Positively hallucinogenic.

Having lived a sheltered childhood, born and raised in the sticks, I hit the road at 20 to find America. Rumors that I lived as a hobo for years are false. I did, however, do some undercover research, as a writer, into the hobo life. There's a difference.

My turn of luck came one summer day when I happened upon a small Nevada town built entirely of neon. Reno. Being smarter than the average hobo, I used the somewhat looser restrictions on human behavior in Nevada to my advantage and soon had a place to stay and a new set of clothes.

So I was looking sharp—shaved, showered, and well fed—when I put my first silver dollar in a slot machine. The second to last silver dollar I had, all that was left after I tipped the barber.

At the front of the machine was a window through which three reels of symbols could be seen. Licking my lips tentatively, I wrapped my hand tightly around the ball at the end of the handle and gave a pull.

The reels spun so that the symbols upon them became a blur. The first reel came to a stop. Cherries. Then the second reel stopped. Cherries. Then the third began to slow down. Oranges, lemons . . . *cherries!* All three of the reels had stopped at cherries.

The machine began to convulse with sound and soon let loose with a gorgeous gush of coins. The person playing the machine next to me shouted, "Jackpot!"

I was trying to catch the silver dollars in a baseball cap I hurriedly "borrowed" from the fellow who'd screamed.

Next thing I knew, a casino employee had me by the elbow and was leading me into a back room to write me a check. Not only were slot machines the pulse of the room—and perhaps the most beautiful thing I had ever seen that didn't involve a well-turned ankle—but they were lucrative as well.

My days of hopping freight trains were through. I would be doing no more research into hobo life. By the following year I had moved back east and set up shop in New Jersey, not far from the boardwalk of Atlantic City.

In the casinos there were thousands of slot machines, each one looking to be played by me.

As silver-dollar slot machines slowly but steadily went the way of the silver dollar, I learned how to counter the casinos' natural advantage by carefully selecting where and when I played the slots.

I learned not to sit at the same machine for hour after hour—unless I was making a steady profit—but to keep my eyes and ears open so that, when I played a machine, the odds of making money were better than normal. I became known as "lucky."

Now, don't get me wrong. That first jackpot in Reno, that was luck. But for the 20-some years since then, I have transformed "one-armed bandits" into one-armed providers. Now I'm going to share my secrets.

I don't want you to think I'm some sort of genius. If that had been the case, I wouldn't have been riding in boxcars to begin with—you don't meet the nicest people there. No, I am of average intelligence, but I'm a good listener.

I didn't invent these strategies. They are the accumulation of years of listening and learning. I've not only learned more than 20 ways to increase my chances of winning at the slots, but I've also learned the background and mechanics of slot machines—truly the most fabulous machine designed for fun and profit in the history of Western Civilization.

A LOTTA ONE-ARMED BANDITS

The so-called one-armed bandits were already doing great business back in the late 1970s when I discovered them, but today, at the dawn of the 21st century, slot machines are more popular than ever.

Check out these statistics: In 1960 there were 16,067 slot machines in the state of Nevada. By 1980 that number had grown to close to 80,000. Today the number approaches 200,000. That's a lot of one-armed bandits!

In 1982, according to the Nevada Gaming Commission and the Atlantic City Casino Hotel Association, slot machines accounted for less than half the total earnings of the casinos in Las Vegas and Atlantic City. Today, however, approximately two-thirds of the casinos' income comes from slot machines.

According to the New Jersey Casino Control Commission, Atlantic City, New Jersey, has 32,786 slot machines within its city limits. The most slots at any given establishment is 4,223, at Trump Plaza. While more than 95 percent of the casinos in the city offer $100 slot machines, only half of them still have nickel slots.

Experts will tell you that, if you're smart, you have a whole lot better chance of making money playing blackjack than you do playing the slots. Sure you do, if you want to count cards—which, if you're not an air-traffic controller, is more stressful than your job.

Slot players are a more relaxed crowd.

They would like to make some money, for sure—but they aren't necessarily willing to take a graduate course in how to do it. Well, this is no graduate course, but in a fun way it will tell you everything you need to know to maximize your chances of winning at the slots.

First, we're going to go through a quick rundown of popular slot machine strategies along with some information that, though not necessarily strategic, could be placed under the column Slot Machine Wisdom.

We'll go through the various situations you might find yourself in while playing slots, and what to do for each of them. We'll look at what's legal and what isn't when it comes to slots, and finally, we're going to hear firsthand from a multitude of slot players, each of whom went from being a loser to being a winner after learning an important lesson about playing the slots, or sometimes about gambling in general.

At the back of the book, for you history buffs, is a history of the slot machine, from its earliest days in the taverns of 19th-century San Francisco to the row after row of computerized machines we find in the modern casino.

CHAPTER ONE
IT'S NOT A JOKE

I know what some of you are saying: "Slot machine strategy! That's a joke; there's no such thing as slot machine strategy. You put your coin in, you pull the arm, and you take your chances. How can you be strategic about that?"

Well, it's a good question. And here's the answer. There are lots of ways to improve your chances of winning, whether it be:

- Determining which machine to play
- Knowing how long to play each machine
- Deciding how much money to risk with every play
- Knowing which casino you should play in
- Understanding which cities' casinos you should play in
- And much more

There are also special strategies when it comes to playing in slot machine tournaments, and for playing progressive jackpot machines. You'll learn what they are later.

IMPROVING YOUR CHANCES OF WINNING

Observing slots players in any casino reveals that people behave toward their slot machines much as they do toward members of the opposite sex. Some players find a machine that they like and they stick with it for a long time.

That's called "steaming."

These people tend to play very quickly, and they think that, if they play a single machine for long enough, they're bound to win the jackpot. Of course, some of them do. But most, as they say, just feed the kitty.

Others prefer to flit from machine to machine like a bee gathering pollen from flower after flower. They never play the same machine for more than three to five pulls; then they move on. As in life, promiscuity at the slot machines is profitable only if taste and discretion are shown.

Of course, any player who has stuck with one machine for hour after hour—falling deeply into the hole before hitting a jackpot and going home a big winner—will swear up and down that this is the way to go.

But the buzzing-bee method is the more profitable of the two in the long run. The trick, to put it mildly, is to determine which machines to flit to when you flit. The first thing that you should determine is the location of the machines that offer the best odds.

Find them and stick with them. Casinos that offer the "loosest" machines—that is, the machines that give you the best return on your dollar—often advertise the fact. Work under the assumption that any machine that doesn't brag about its user-friendliness is casino-friendly.

ALL MACHINES 95 PERCENT IN THE PLAYERS' FAVOR

A frequently asked question among casino neophytes is: "What does the sign mean when it says, ALL MACHINES 95 PERCENT IN THE PLAYERS' FAVOR?" Not all casinos post these signs, but many do, and it's important that you understand what they mean.

The sign may be worded to be purposefully confusing, but it's something to look for nonetheless. The sign's sentiments could best be rephrased as, "All machines 5 percent in the house's favor."

What the sign means is that, for every 100 units you play, you can expect, on average, 95 units back. Though the sign isn't as clear as it could be, those odds aren't bad. Some slot machines are set up to give the casino a whopping 16 percent advantage.

CHOOSING THE CORRECT MACHINE TO PLAY

Not everyone goes to the casino with the same objective in mind. Some folks are looking to make a zillion dollars so they can buy an island in the South Pacific where they can sip cool drinks and never work again.

Some players are looking to make just enough to pay for their vacation, or maybe buy a new car. Some, of course, are happy to break even, content that they got to play the game and they didn't lose too much.

Depending on which of these categories you belong to, there are slot machines geared toward you. For example, if you want to make a zillion dollars, then we recommend you stick to jackpot-only machines.

These machines don't pay off very often. There are few small payouts, but generally when they do pay, you get to buy an island in the South Pacific. On the other hand, there are machines that don't have a super-big jackpot but pay off more frequently in smaller amounts, usually less than 18 coins.

There are far more players in the latter category. They need the positive encouragement of frequent payouts in order to continue playing. It takes a certain amount of guts to crank coin after coin into a machine that fails to respond in the hope that, after hours of trying, you'll finally hit it big.

AVOID DARK CORNERS

Casinos will put the loosest machines, the slots that pay off the best, where the most people are apt to see them. Yet they don't want the loosest machines to be in the hustle and bustle of crossroads of walking aisles, for example.

There are two considerations for the casinos here. They want the winners of big jackpots to be seen and heard by as many people as possible, but they also want to reward long-time players as much as possible, while burning the fellow who puts in a coin and runs. They know that folks who are going to play the slots for hour after hour are not going to want to sit at machines in a major thoroughfare. These people want to be inside the slots parlor a bit. Ah, but because winners need to be seen and heard, experienced slots players avoid the machines that are too far off the beaten path.

So the greatest majority of loose machines are just off the thoroughfare, where they can be seen and heard, but are still appealing to veteran players who play long hours—those who "play their dues," so to speak.

Casinos, after all, don't want players to win their jackpots in a dark corner where no one will be able to see them. For the same reason that a jackpot winner is forced to walk around the lobby of the hotel carrying a fake check the size of a billboard, jackpot winners often find themselves near the hub of the casino's circulatory system.

There will be those who swear up and down that casinos do not work this way. The casinos, they will say, buy slot machines by the row, install them, and collect the money. They insist there is no deep thinking involved.

I would be inclined to agree if it were true that all slot machines are manufactured identically, but that's not the case. The truth of the matter is that there are tight and loose machines—and the casinos themselves get to request from the manufacturer how many of each they want.

Why? Obviously, so that the machines can be placed to give the casino maximum strategic advantage. To do it any other way would be stupid, and that is one thing that casinos are not.

One thing to keep in mind, however: Just because the loosest machines are put in popular spots doesn't mean that all machines in popular spots are loose. For reasons evident to those with an instinct for capitalism, there are a lot more tight machines than loose ones.

There is an exception to this rule: Casinos don't like to put loose slots near the table games, where players are expected to "think."

BIG BERTHA BE TIGHT

It has been my experience that Big Bertha slots—those gigantic machines usually placed at the entranceway to the slot section of the casino—are tighter.

If you can't resist just one coin, so you can feel the heft of that gigantic arm, I understand. But anyone who would attach himself to a Big Bertha for any length of time is looking to lighten his pockets. The fact is that most people who play the Big Bertha only put in one coin. She is so big that it would be difficult, and damn conspicuous, to play her for hour after hour. Since her specialty is extreme short-term players, the casino can burn each and every one of them without worrying about losing anyone to a competing casino.

READ THE MACHINE

There are many different types of slot machines, varying both by casino and within a single casino—and they all seem to have different rules. Therefore, and this is important, always read the instructions and the rules on the machine before you start to play.

Don't be heartbroken to see that you've lined up the cherries just the way you should to win the six zillion dollars, but you didn't insert the correct number of quarters, so instead your payoff is 25 bucks. Those tears can be extremely bitter.

FOR FUN, KEEP THE STAKES LOW

If you're going to play for "fun," then keep the stakes low. Don't play the dollar machines unless you're ready to lose a few bucks. Players who like the action and don't want the stress of worrying about losing can make 20 bucks' worth of nickels last a long time, and have every bit as much fun as they would if they were playing with silver dollars.

DO LARGE CASINOS PAY OFF BETTER?

It's commonly believed that slot machines in large casinos pay off better than those in the smaller places, but research has proven that this isn't necessarily true. The looseness of a casino's machines is determined by the amount of effort the casino is putting into attracting slots players to its parlors. Some casinos are known for their blackjack tables, and others for their sports book. Still others are known for their slots, and both small and large casinos fit into this category.

The machines' rate of payoff is set at the factory before the machine is even delivered. Even though the purchaser of the machine—that is, the casino—has input as to the specific payoff rate of each machine, all machines must be set inside a payoff range that is stipulated by state law.

BEWARE OF SPEED-UP GAMES

Casinos are constantly looking for ways to suck up more of your money. And over the years they have grown very good at it. One example of this is the slot machine that "rewards" you for playing fast. Beware!

There are different gimmicks involved, but the point is that these machines increase the potential jackpot if you play a certain number of coins within a certain amount of time. In other words, the faster you play, the faster you lose.

One machine I saw in Las Vegas involved a diver. On the top of the machine was a plastic man in skin-diving equipment. Each reel had a symbol that said DIVE. Each time the symbol DIVE came up one or more times, the man moved farther down a tube, getting deeper into the ocean.

If you were to hit a jackpot, the deeper the diver was, the bigger the jackpot would be. This sounds like a pretty fair incentive—except for one thing. The whole mechanism was on a timer. Each 1 minute and 40 seconds, the diver returned to the top of the tube.

Plus there was a big clock on the front of the machine that counted down from 1:40 to 0:00. The natural instinct of the players is thus to hurry up and play as many coins as quickly as they can so that, if they hit, the diver is well down the tube.

Trouble is, the machine doesn't hit any more often than any other machine (it may even hit less often). And if you don't hit, it just doesn't make any difference how far down the tube the little diver is. This is just a way for the casino to get the player to think less and wager more.

SLOW DOWN AND PAY ATTENTION

Speaking of speed-up games, it's a good idea to not play too fast no matter which machine you're using. The reason for this is that you may hit a jackpot and not even know it. And that is the saddest of all possible stories.

When a jackpot is hit, a bell is supposed to go off on your machine to alert you that you're about to come into some cash—and alert everyone in your vicinity, for that matter. The casino wants as many people as possible to know that a jackpot has been won.

Some jackpots pay off partially in the coin tray, so that you get the thrill of the coins rushing out of the machine, while the remainder is paid to you by a nearby attendant. That was the case with my initial Reno jackpot.

Sometimes the attendant is responsible for paying off the entire jackpot, and no money goes into the tray on your machine. Only rarely does the machine award you the entire jackpot. That would involve a wheelbarrow's worth of coins.

The point is, if the bell on your machine happens to be broken, you might quickly play another coin, negating the jackpot you just—or rather, could have—won.

So unless you want to take the risk of winning the jackpot but not getting any money, always pause and look at the symbols that have come up on your reels before you play another coin.

If three bells wins the jackpot and you're looking at three bells but your machine isn't reacting properly, *stop right then and there and contact an attendant before you proceed.*

PLAYING MORE THAN ONE MACHINE; OR, THE CASINO GIVETH AND THE CASINO TAKETH AWAY

Many players like to play two slot machines at the same time. Realizing this, it's a strategy of the casinos—as part of their slot mix, which they claim doesn't exist—to alternate loose and tight machines along a row.

This way players who are using two machines at the same time usually have one that's paying off and one that isn't. The one that isn't ends up getting fed the winnings from the one that is.

If you find that your right hand is giving away what your left hand is taking, find a row of slots that's fairly empty and try playing every other machine.

MAKE FRIENDS

There aren't as many change makers as there once were in casinos, because automatic change machines have been installed. But as you probably already know, these machines refuse to take any bill that has as much as a wrinkle in it. Until the change machines are perfected, then, change people will still be wandering around the slot machine sections of the casino, taking bills and handing out coins.

And they are a bored lot, easy to approach and easy to befriend. Change people are also an observant group, and probing their minds before you start playing can't hurt. Don't be afraid to ask things like, "Say, which one of these machines is ready to hit the jackpot?"

Or, "Any machines around here I should avoid?"

Be discreet, because change people won't want to start dispensing winning advice if their boss is watching. Every once in a while, though, you're liable to pick up a tidbit that leads to winning.

(It's good casino etiquette that, if you so accept a piece of advice from a change person and you do hit it big, give a nice tip. You'll feel even better.)

ETIQUETTE

A brief note on slot machine etiquette. It's considered bad form to play more than two machines at the same time. If it's five o'clock in the morning and there are few people in the joint, then you can get away with it.

Other than that, expect to find offended people forcing their way into your domain if you attempt to play more than two machines at the same time.

Now, three is taboo, but two is normal. Lots of people play two machines at the same time. But even here there's a right way and a wrong way to do it.

You don't stand between the slot machines, but rather sit down in front of one. You don't play the machines at the same time, but rather one at a time.

When you win, leave a few coins in the tray at the bottom of the machine. This will discourage others from trying to sit down next to you and take your machine.

Some casinos have a regular policy of allowing only one machine to a customer. Others restrict players to one machine only when the slot parlors are extremely crowded.

If this is the case, the casino will either have personnel come around announcing the rule, or signs will announce it. Either way, give up the second machine if the casino tells you to.

If you refuse, you'll usually be asked to leave.

RESERVING YOUR FAVORITE MACHINE

Here's another dilemma that slot machine players sometimes find themselves in. You're playing a hot machine, it has been giving out a solid 125 percent return on your investment, and it's ripe to hit the big jackpot.

Other players, none of whom is doing anywhere near as well as you, are eyeing your machine enviously. All is well with the world—except for one minor point. You have to visit the rest room. The second you cash in and leave, your machine will be swooped upon by the hungry masses.

What do you do?

The good news is that, in most casinos, you don't have to give up your favorite slot machine to go to the bathroom. If you plan to be away from the machine for only a few minutes, a casino employee will usually be willing to close down the machine temporarily while you're away.

If you want to have the machine shut down while you're away for more than 10 minutes—say, for your dinner break—then casinos won't be nearly as cooperative. If the casino is empty, you could probably get away with it—although a healthy tip would be expected.

WINNING BIG AND ITS CONSEQUENCES

Remember, if you do win a million-dollar jackpot on a slot machine, be prepared to become a bit of a celebrity. Understandably, casinos like to use their winners for public relations purposes.

The casino will want as many people as possible to know about you and your good fortune. Among other things, you will probably be asked to parade around the casino entrance—and maybe around the hotel lobby, if there is one—while carrying a six-foot-long check with your million-dollar jackpot in bold letters.

These humongous checks, by the way, are not negotiable. You'll be issued a normal-sized check, too, and that's the one that you endorse and take to the bank.

A MATTER OF LUCK

Will you win the big jackpot at a casino in your lifetime? Maybe. Probably not. It's a lot like catching a foul ball at the ballpark. Lifelong fans have never caught one, while newcomers have caught two in the same inning. If it happened all the time, guys like me wouldn't make the papers when we hit our jackpots, and we do.

The way to make money at the slots is to simply rake in more than you put in over the long run. If you win a big jackpot, which in this day and age can amount to millions of dollars, that's gravy.

For a further discussion of these principles, and others not yet discussed, be sure to read chapter 11 for many "Profiles of Slot Machine Winners."

CHAPTER TWO
TYPES OF SLOT
MACHINES

Here's a quick review of the various types of slot machines you might encounter during your wagering travels. The biggest difference between slot machines in the modern casino is that some are mechanical and others, the new ones, are computerized.

What's the difference?

Well, for one thing, the mechanical machines, most of which are electronically operated, have actual reels with actual symbols on them. They really spin and they really stop at random.

Because this is true, we can figure out precisely what the odds are of any particular outcome.

In the old days, before mechanical slot machines became electronic, pulling the handle actually engaged the reels. Players figured they could alter the outcome by pulling the handle softly or firmly. Even then this could only be done with extremely limited success. Today it would be impossible.

Today's electronic slots, though still mechanical, operate on electronic impulses. The handle merely activates the impulse, and the impulse gets the reels moving. In fact, in most machines these days it's no longer even necessary to pull the handle in order to engage the reels. A button on the front of the machine accomplishes the same thing.

GIVE-AND-TAKE CYCLES

Mechanical slot machines—and some folks still prefer to play them, even though they're growing increasingly rare in this increasingly computerized world—have periods where they pay off more than they receive and periods where they receive more than they pay out. The "take" cycles are just a little bit longer than the "give" cycles, as you might imagine.

If mechanical slot machines were set to be in either payoff mode or take mode for intervals of varying length, they would be easy to figure out. You would merely avoid playing machines that had recently paid off.

In other words, every time you received a payoff you would switch machines and stick somebody else with that machine's take cycle. Ah, but this is not the way slot machines are set up. They're more complicated than that.

They do pay off during their take cycles, and take during their payoff cycles; they just do it in varying ratios so that over the long run they hit their payoff specifications. So even with machines into which you lose money, there's apt to come a time when you're ahead.

The question is, will you blow the money you've made or will you make more? Is the machine in its give cycle or its take cycle? Best advice there is: Don't ask. If you're ahead, but not as far ahead as you were a few minutes before, stop using the machine and move to another. You may never get another chance—on that machine, anyway—to be ahead.

The newfangled computerized machines that are cropping up more and more in casinos have no reels. What you're looking at is a computer screen with pictures of reels on it. The computer's operating chip determines where the "reels" stop and how often and in what amounts the payoffs come in.

So in chapter 7, when I describe the methods by which we determine the odds of a particular outcome, remember that I'm discussing mechanical slots only. These lessons are not wasted when it comes to computerized slots, however, because the programs that run the computerized machines are inevitably based on the physical realities of mechanical slot probabilities. We'll discuss computerized slots in detail in chapter 8.

SINGLE- AND MULTIPLE-COIN MACHINES

The simplest slot machine still extant in the modern casino is the single-coin slot. These are machines that accept only one coin at a time—that is, one coin per play. These machines do not pay off in large jackpots but are popular because they pay off in smaller amounts more frequently.

Then there are multiple-coin machines. These are machines in which you can bet anywhere from one to (say) four coins per play. Some machines take anywhere from one to six coins. The trick here is that you can only win the really *big* jackpot if you're betting the maximum number of coins per play.

And the payoffs are always affected by the number of coins you've bet. Two cherries when you're betting two

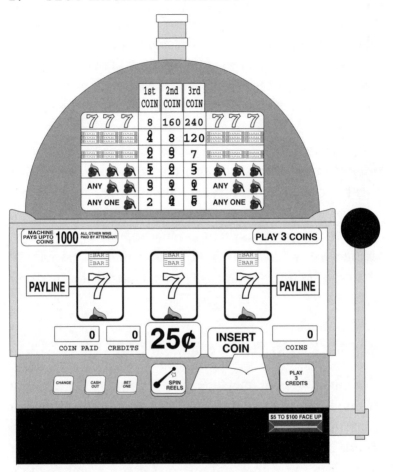

	1st COIN	2nd COIN	3rd COIN	
7 7 7	8	160	240	7 7 7
BAR BAR BAR	4	8	120	BAR BAR BAR
BAR BAR BAR	9	9	7	BAR BAR BAR
🍒🍒🍒	5	2	5	🍒🍒🍒
ANY 🍒🍒	9	9	9	ANY 🍒🍒
ANY ONE 🍒	2	4	5	ANY ONE 🍒

MACHINE PAYS UPTO COINS **1000** ALL OTHER WINS PAID BY ATTENDANT   PLAY 3 COINS

PAYLINE   7   7   7   PAYLINE

0	0	**25¢**	INSERT COIN	0
COIN PAID	CREDITS			COINS

CHANGE   CASH OUT   BET ONE   SPIN REELS   PLAY 3 CREDITS

$5 TO $100 FACE UP

coins pays better than twice what two cherries would pay when you're betting one coin. Betting three coins would pay off even better than that, and so forth.

The machines are called "multipliers" because they're able to multiply the payoff by the number of coins you've inserted. If a player plays one coin, hits three cherries, and receives 100 coins, a player who played two coins and got the same three cherries would receive 200 coins. In other words, the machine knew it should multiply the 100 coins by two because two coins had been inserted.

Since most people who play multipliers play the maximum number of coins per play, the casino is playing a subtle game with their heads. Players who wouldn't play dollar slots in a million years because it's "too rich for their blood" will play a four-coin quarter machine and repeatedly play four quarters per play. Go figure.

As we'll learn later, do not assume that the most conservative bet is the least risky over the long run on these machines. Some multiple-coin machines pay out better percentagewise when more than one coin is played. This is partially because these machines are designed to reward the risk, since the casino assumes that most people will see the advantage of taking the maximum risk per play.

There are some multiple-coin machines that pay off on an even scale. The same result that pays off five coins for a one-coin play would pay off ten for a two-coin play and fifteen for a three-coin play. On these machines it makes no difference over the long run if you play one coin per play or three coins per play. Without the incentive to risk more than one coin per play, many players are content to get to the same place more slowly. By adding the incentive of better payoffs for multiple coins per play, casinos have effectively turned quarter machines into dollar machines.

BUY-A-PAY

Buy-a-pay machines can be a lot of fun, as long as you don't find yourself playing one by mistake. Being unpleasantly surprised by a buy-a-pay machine can be a heart-breaking experience.

Buy-a-pay machines work like this: Like the multipliers, they accept anywhere from one to five coins. Usually the number of coins that the machine accepts is the same as the number of different symbols that appear on each of three reels.

Then, if you bet one coin, you win the payoff only if you get three lemons. If you bet two coins, you win if you line up the lemons or the cherries. If you bet three coins, you can line up lemons, cherries, or 7s. Et cetera.

If you bet the maximum, the machines pay off regardless of which symbol it is that lines up.

Here's an example of why it's so important to read all of the instructions on a machine before you start popping coins into it. Buy-a-pay machines have caused a lot of security problems over the years, from angry players who weren't aware that they were on a buy-a-pay machine. They lined up three lemons when they paid only for cherries, and they couldn't believe that they weren't getting a little something.

MULTIPLE-PAYLINE SLOTS

While most slot machines have just one line in the center of the window along which symbols can line up to result in a payoff, there are those in which more than one line counts.

The most common number of payout lines on multiple-payline slots is three or five. They sometimes pay off on the diagonal as well. They're sometimes called "crisscross" machines. If you believe that no game is truly fun unless it has an element of tic-tac-toe in it, then multiple-payline slot machines are for you.

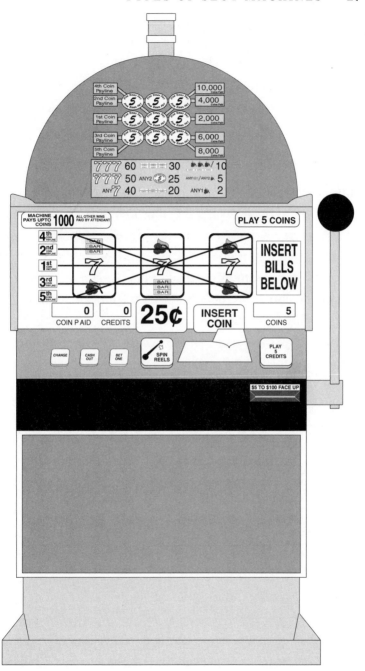

Though a multiple-payline machine may be more fun to play, this is no guarantee that it's a moneymaker. Quite the contrary is often true. The truth is, there are tight multiple-payline machines as well as loose ones, with the range and proportion of each about the same as for single-payline machines.

A multiple-payline slot machine that is also buy-a-pay may offer payouts only on the center line when one coin is played, only on the center line and the one above it when two coins are played, on the center line plus the line above and below it when three coins are played . . . until all variations of the tic-tac-toe board become potential winners when the maximum number of coins is played. As always, though, be sure you know the rules of the game before you start playing it.

Naturally, the casino wants everyone to play the maximum number of coins on each play, so it sweetens the pot a bit for the ultimate risk takers. A one-coin play that brings three cherries might pay 25 coins. The same result might pay 50 coins for a two-coin bet.

Yet if three coins is the maximum the machine takes, a three-coin bet might result in 250 coins when three cherries comes up.

There are a few multiple-payline machines out there that don't give bonuses for playing the maximum number of coins per day, so, as always, read your machine before you play it.

PROGRESSIVE MACHINES

A progressive machine is usually a multiple-coin machine, and sometimes a multiple-payline machine as well. It's different in that its jackpot fluctuates. The amount of the jackpot always appears in lights at the top of the machine, usually in bright red numbers. This jackpot grows and grows until it's hit, and then it resets.

Sometimes, in order to build up tremendous jackpots, casinos will hook up entire banks of slot machines to a single progressive jackpot. Chapter 11 has a lot more information about progressive jackpots and the methods that various successful slots players use in trying to win them. Here are some quick suggestions.

Always play on the machine, or bank of machines, with the largest jackpot. Although it isn't true that the machine with the largest jackpot is more likely to win on the next play than a machine that has recently reset, it *is* true that it's

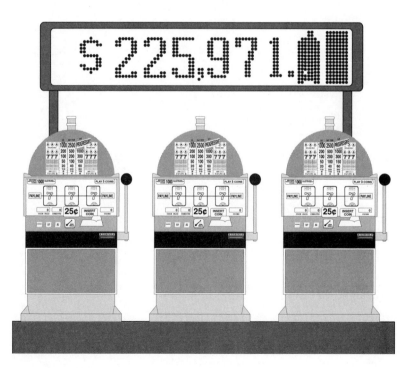

equally likely that both will hit on the next play. This being the case, why not play for the larger amount of money?

As a rule, progressive machines offer the big jackpot only to players who are playing the maximum number of coins. Again, avoid the heartache and know what you're doing.

CHAPTER THREE
MODERN SLOTS

There are slots players who will only play on mechanical slot machines—machines that have no element of computer programming. I asked one slot machine player why she preferred the mechanical machines to the modern ones with computerized payoff rates and video screens.

"I believe in being ripped off honestly," she said. "The mechanical machines are random. You can tell. They stop where they stop. With the computerized game I always get the impression that the machine knows whether I'm winning or losing. It can count. It's not that I don't trust the machine. I just don't trust the man back at the factory who is programming those things."

As for me, it isn't that I don't trust the computer slot machines. I suspect that the same guy who programs the com-

puter games is calibrating the mechanisms of the mechanical ones.

If any evidence exists that computerized slot machines
have a worse payoff rate than mechanical slot machines, I
don't know about it. You can get a good or bad machine in
both categories, and the range of payout rates inside each
group is wider than any difference between the two groups.

So if you prefer modern technology and computers and
the like, it's no longer necessary to play a real slot machine.
You don't have to pull a handle. Video slots take your coin
and then show you a video of a slot machine. You win
some, you lose some—but somehow you're missing out on
the actual movement, the spinning, of a real slot machine.
It's not the same.

The video machines don't offer just slot action, however. A variety of games, such as blackjack, keno, and
poker, is offered. Still, why play a machine that simulates
poker when a real game of poker is 50 feet away? Maybe
that works for really shy people, but not for me.

Video slots are nothing new, so I guess they're here to
stay. Video slots, in fact, first appeared more than 30 years
ago. Though a prototype for a video slot was built in 1966,
the machines didn't take off in popularity until the 1980s,
with video poker being the most popular.

(If you do play video poker, by the way, lay off the double-
or-nothing option after you win. It's one-card draw for all
the marbles. The machine draws first, and it seems like it always puts up a King or an Ace to beat. You get a Three.)

If you're going to play video slot machines that simulate
the rules of other casino games, always be sure that you're

familiar with the rules of the particular game before you use that machine.

In other words, don't play the poker machine unless you know how to play poker, don't play the keno machine unless you know how to play keno, and don't play the blackjack machine unless you know how to play blackjack. You'll be called upon to make the same sorts of decisions while playing the video game that you would if you were at an actual gaming table playing the real thing. Thus it's your skill at the particular game that will help determine whether or not you go home a winner.

COMFORT

One thing that the makers of video slots are hip to is comfort. During the entire time that mechanical slots were manufactured, no one ever thought about the comfort of the player, who either used the machine while standing up or sat on the bar stool that the casino provided.

The makers of video slots, on the other hand, often sell the machine and its chair as a unit, and the chair usually has a back on it and swivels. If you're prone to sore backs, like me, such little things can make all of the difference in the world.

POKER MATIC

The slot machine business changed forever in 1970 when a machine called the "Poker Matic" was introduced in casinos all over Nevada. Sure, there had been a machine that simulated a game of poker as far back as 1901, but this was the first machine that paid out like any other slot machine. The Poker Matic machines were immediately popular, so naturally the phenomenon expanded until other casino games were represented.

Pretty soon it was hard to think of a game offered in a casino for which there wasn't a slot machine. Machines that played craps were around by 1974. In 1979 a machine called Big Red Keno was introduced. Players could play anywhere from one to four coins, and used a light pen to select the numbers. (More about keno machines in a moment.)

In 1985 the first slot machines that simulated horse races were manufactured. The most popular was called Derby, which was manufactured by Sigma. Ten players could play at once, and stood around a model track with little horses that actually went around. A player could bet anywhere from one to twenty coins on one of five horses per race.

By 1985 you could play the imaginary horses in a video game, which used a laser disc player to race five horses on a video screen. The best part was there was an announcer who called the race, and the sound effects offered the noise of Thoroughbred hooves on the track.

POKER PAYOUTS

Here are the typical payouts for various hands for a poker machine that accepts anywhere from one to five coins per play:

- One pair of Jacks or better (that is, one pair of Queens, Kings, or Aces) earns your money back no matter how many coins you play.

- A hand of two pairs will double your bet, no matter how many coins you play.
- Three of a kind triples your bet, and a straight quadruples it.
- A flush plays 5 to 1, and a full house 8 to 1.
- Four of a kind pays off 25 to 1, and a straight flush pays off at 50 to 1.

On multiple-coin machines remember that it's always your best bet to risk the maximum number of coins per play, because the machine rewards the maximum play. In this case the reward comes when you're dealt a royal flush on the machine. For a one-, two-, three-, or four-coin play, the royal flush pays off at 250 to 1. However, if you bet five coins and get a royal flush, the payoff is a tremendous 4,000 coins, or 800 to 1. In other words, if you play this machine and you don't risk five coins per play, you're passing up the chance to win the big bonus.

Some machines don't pay for a pair of Jacks or better. On these machines you need to get at least two pairs before the machine pays anything at all. If you have a choice, for obvious reasons, play on a machine that gives you your money back for a high pair.

As a rule, the profit margin for the casinos on machines that don't recognize a high pair as a winning hand are much higher than on those that do.

Video poker games are more interactive than straight-forward mechanical slots. Most poker games use the rules of draw poker, so after you're dealt your initial hand you're given a choice of which cards you want to hold on to and which you want to replace.

On a regular slot machine, when you lose you have no one to blame but the machine. If you lose at video poker, there's a chance that things might have been different if you had played your cards differently.

KENO MACHINES

Keno machines feature the numbers 1 through 80. On each play, 10 of these numbers are chosen by the machine. You must guess ahead of time which of the numbers will be chosen. You can guess anywhere from 2 to 10 numbers. If you guess two numbers, both of them must come up for, typically, a 14-to-1 payout. Three out of three pays 40 to 1. Four out of four pays 100 to 1. Five out of five pays 800 to 1. Six out of six pays 7,760 to 1. Eight out of eight pays 8,000 to 1. Nine out of nine pays 9,000 to 1. And ten out of ten pays 10,000 to 1. If you guess three or more numbers, you don't have to get them all correct in order to collect. Two out of three pays 2 to 1. Pick nine numbers and have four of them come up and you get your money back. Pick 9 out of 10 and the payoff is 4,800 to 1.

MONEY CHANGERS

One item that the modern slot machine has that previous models lacked is the paper-money changer. This innovation was introduced to vending machines at about the same time. Depending on which neck of the woods you're playing in, the machine might change anything from $1 to $100 bills.

As I mentioned before, the money-changing machines built into the modern slots are, unfortunately, no better than the ones you might otherwise be used to. One little fold in the corner of a bill and the damn thing spits it back. Assuming you have a bill that's adequately flat, you feed it into the slot, push the CASH OUT button, and the correct number of coins comes out—eager, of course, to be fed back in.

SLOTS PLAYER CARD

A Slots Player Card is usually made of plastic and slips into your slot machine as you play it. In this way you can accrue premium points on your card, depending on how much you play, and earn gifts and perks from the casino. A light player might earn a T-shirt. A heavy player might get free dinner for two. The highest plateau gets a free room at the hotel.

Of course, the card comes with a downside. If you're working a system that you don't necessarily want the casino to know about, having a Slots Player Card could ruin your day. The card keeps track for the casino of which machines you're using and when, along with how much money you're playing, and winning, at each machine.

Also, be very careful to reclaim your card when you leave a machine.

Finally, if the person tugging the handle next to you is trying to make you believe that you win more if you use the card, don't believe it. You will win, or lose, precisely what you would have won or lost without using the card. However, the card almost always comes with perks for those who play a lot. In this sense it's to your advantage to use the card. If you aren't concerned with your privacy, why not take the perks?

TOURNAMENTS

If you enjoy playing the slots, then you should think about participating in a slots tournament. Casinos that host them will be more than glad to put you on their mailing list, so you'll be notified when they hold their next event.

For the tournament an area of the casino is set aside, with the number of reserved machines corresponding to the number of players who have entered. You give the tournament an entrance fee—which can range anywhere from $25 to $400, depending on the size of the event.

You then don't have to put any money into the machines. Modern slots are used and are each set with a predetermined number of credits, so each player starts off at the same place.

The event is then held in "sessions," which are 15- to 20-minute stints during which you play on one machine and try to accumulate as many credits as you can. Players at the tournaments never use the handle, but rather keep their fingers steadily pressing at the spin button in order to spin the reels as many times as possible during the session.

Those who accrue the highest number of credits move on to the next session. Players continue to be eliminated until there is a winner, who receives the grand prize.

INTERNET SLOTS

Before you play the slots on the Internet, there are a few things you'll want to determine. (Actually, many of these tips hold true for any Web site that requires your credit-card number.)

How attractive is the site? A fly-by-night operation will often have a fly-by-night look. Are there warnings and assurances regarding the confidentiality of the information they're requesting from you? There should be.

Is it easy to contact the proprietor of the site? Is there a phone number? An address to write to—one that isn't just a post office box? Are they e-mail accessible? If so, write them a note and see how quickly they answer. In other words, make sure someone is home.

And finally, if you plan to put any money at all into on-line slots and you have the slightest doubt about the site at which you're playing, call the Better Business Bureau and make sure everything is on the up and up.

CHAPTER FOUR
LEGALITIES AND
ILLEGALITIES

Here's something that might have happened to you. If not, come along. It'll be an adventure.

You're in a state in which gambling is illegal—a state in which there are no Indian reservations and no loopholes. Let's say you're walking through an urban area one evening. You pass an amiable tavern with dim light, a pool table, and the ball game on TV.

A sudden thirst grips you, so you duck inside for a couple. On your way to the rest room you happen to peek into a small back room and there, much to your delight, is a row of five slot machines. Should you play? I decided to find out.

I searched urban sidewalks from coast to coast. Well, not really. I actually hit pay dirt on only the third saloon to envelop me in its warmth. It was a Sunday at noontime. The bartender was alone, and he turned out to also be the proprietor. Best of all, I explained who I was and he told me he'd give me the truth, as long as I didn't use his name.

"That would be very bad," he said gravely. So I'm sworn to secrecy. We don't want Mr. X to receive any cosmetic surgery via blowtorch, do we? No, we do not.

So Mr. X gave me the skinny. Here it is: Don't play illegal machines. It's a total rip-off.

"First of all, there aren't any machines to compete with mine," he said. "If you want to play a slot machine and you live in the neighborhood, it's either play mine or drive all night to a casino."

Do illegal machines ever pay out?

"Sure, but small payouts only. No jackpots, and the thing keeps more than half the coins it receives," said our owner as he wiped circles off the bar with a rag.

But how much money do these machines actually take in?

"You'd be surprised. People will go in there in groups and every time two or three quarters come out they whoop with joy, totally forgetting that they just put in eight. I mean, my machines don't stay as busy as the ones in Atlantic City. People come in here for things other than the slots, but it's not like they're gathering dust back there either."

I know it's hard not to drop a coin into every slot you see. I feel your pain. But the simple rule of thumb is that whenever you play slots, you should make sure that the slots are, in the Shakespearean sense, the *thing*.

For those of you who don't know your Macbeths from your McMuffins, this means you should play slot machines only where the slots themselves are the primary activity. If it's a matter of, "Hey, they have a slot machine, too," don't play. The people on either side of you when you're dropping your coins should be there to play slots, not to see the show or eat the food. Go to the places where the slot players go.

Okay, here's a pop quiz: You're in a sports bar and everyone is watching 14 different football games on a series of large-screen televisions—and there's a slot machine over in the corner between the pay phone and the cigarette machine. Do you play it? *No!*

Follow-up question: You're eating in a Chinese restaurant just off the beaten path in Vegas. You ask for the rest room and they point to a curtained exit in the back. Behind the curtain a narrow staircase heads steeply downward. At the bottom of the stairs, dimly lit but visible, are two doors; there's a little pink umbrella on one, blue on the other. There's also a tall ashtray with sand in its top, a mirror, an ink painting on rice paper, and the most beautiful slot machine you have ever seen, shaped like a pagoda and playing a music-box version of "Sukiyaki." Do you put a coin in? Answer: Nay.

Here's another: Picture this. You're cruising just outside of Lovelock, Nevada, in your red T-bird convertible. Being a healthy quaffer of the world's finest lager, you find yourself in need of a personal pit stop. So you pull into a full-service Exxon for gas. After you TCB, you go into the garage and there, oily and grease-stained, with art deco fins and a grill that screams 1958, is a slot machine with big neon letters on it: C-H-E-V-Y. Do you play? Answer: Walk away quickly. Flee.

One last question: You have a big ol' sack of laundry so you head to the Laundromat. And there, way in the back, right between the coin-operated soap powder dispenser and the folding counter, is a slot machine with a picture of Marilyn Monroe on it. A subway grate is blowing up her dress, and the arm you pull is Marilyn's left arm. Do you play? Answer: Nyuh uh!

Oh, all right. Maybe just one coin.

THE WORLD'S LARGEST SLOT MACHINE

The world's largest slot machine is 10 feet wide, 9 feet tall, and 5 feet across. It resides at Bill's Lake Tahoe Casino. Built by Bally, the humongous slot machine takes silver dollars. It was originally named Big Barney but changed its name and gender in 1987, becoming Billie Jean.

A LEGAL WARNING

These days just about everybody knows that if you own a bar and you want to put a slot machine in your establishment, you'd better be in Nevada. Otherwise you—like Mr. X—are looking to be arrested. It's against the law.

But what if you want to put a slot machine inside your private home? You know, just for fun. Are you still risking arrest? The answer once again depends on where you are.

In Alabama, Connecticut, Hawaii, Indiana, Nebraska, Rhode Island, South Carolina, and Tennessee you would be breaking the law. It is illegal to own a slot machine in these states no matter what the circumstances.

The only legal slot machines in these states are the ones on the land of an Indian reservation, where the resident tribe has fewer limitations on its moneymaking (and -losing) options.

In the following states you may own any slot machine you choose as long as you keep it inside your home: Alaska,

Arizona, Arkansas, Kentucky, Louisiana, Maine, Minnesota, Nevada (duh!), New Mexico, Ohio, Texas, Utah, Virginia, and West Virginia.

In these states it is legal to own a slot machine in your own home as long as it is twenty-five years old or older: California, Delaware, Illinois, Iowa, Maryland, Michigan, Mississippi, Montana, New Hampshire, North Carolina, North Dakota, Oklahoma, Washington, Wisconsin, and Wyoming. The machine must have been built before 1950 in Georgia, Idaho, Kansas, and New York. The year is 1941 in Pennsylvania and South Dakota, 1952 in the District of Columbia, 1954 in Vermont, and 1968 in Oregon. In Florida the machine must be 20 years older or more. In Massachusetts, New Jersey, and Missouri it must be 30 years old or older. In Colorado it is legal only if the machine was made before 1984.

THE TAX MAN COMETH

You would think that with all the money slot machines make for casinos these days, the Internal Revenue Service would lay off the fortunate players who hit a jackpot.

But no.

If you win a jackpot of greater than $1,200, you are required by law to report it to the IRS as income. It isn't necessary for you to pay tax on it then and there. But your total tax for the year will be figured based on your total income, of which your jackpot earnings will be a part.

The casinos know what to do, and it's their responsibility, not yours, to take care of the paperwork. If you win, a casino employee will, with your help, fill out and file a W-2G form.

In order for the casinos to fill out the form, they're going to need proof that you are who you say you are, since they don't want to be a party to tax fraud.

It's therefore essential that you bring proper identification with you whenever you go to the casinos to gamble. At least if you want to go home with your money, and we assume you do.

If you don't have proper ID, the casino will hold your money for you and release it to you after you return with ID. Proper identification shouldn't be a problem for most people: A credit card, bank card, or driver's license usually does the trick, and most of us carry these things as a matter of course.

This is true only if you're a citizen of the United States, however. If you're a foreigner gambling in the U.S. and you win a slot machine jackpot of greater than $1,200, you'll have the appropriate amount of tax taken out of your winnings right then and there. The amount depends on your nation of origin and can be as high as 30 percent.

If you're Canadian, the amount that will be taken out of your winnings is 15 percent.

I know what you're saying: If they can tax my winnings, why can't I deduct my losses? The answer is that you *can* deduct your losses. You just have to include enough documentation to convince any potential auditor that your losses were real.

What sort of documents?

Well, everything would be easy if slot machines gave receipts, but they don't. In terms of the actual amount of money you lost at a machine, the IRS is simply going to have to take your word. Your job is to prove to the IRS auditor that you were where you said you were when you said you were there, and that you were doing what you said you were doing—namely, losing money in the slot machines.

So keep your receipts from your hotel and the parking lot. This will prove that you were in the correct place at the correct time.

If you are audited and your declared losses at the slot machines are questioned, you should be able to deluge your auditor with documentation. Some have even suggested making a note of the names of all of the casino and hotel employees you come in contact with. Your auditor cannot, in good faith, reject your deduction until she investigates the legitimacy of your documents. With a time-consuming task like this in front of her, she may lose the urge to question your deduction in the first place.

CHAPTER FIVE
OLD WIVES' TALES

Here are a couple of longtime "tips" best filed in the Old Wives' Tale department. The first is that you should only play slot machines on Friday and Saturday nights. The theory goes that the machines have already earned their quota for the week by the weekend, so they're less stingy at that time.

It's true that there are more winners on the weekend than there are on weekdays, but that's because there are more players on the weekend. I also believe that casinos would like to have winners screaming with joy more frequently per machine when the place is crowded—because the winning feeling then takes over the very souls of that many more prospective slots players—but there is no truth to the rumor that machines know what day it is, or that they make all the money they can during the week so they can dump it into the pockets of weekend-only players. While it's absolutely true that there are tight machines and loose machines, they don't switch back and forth. The rate of return is preset in the machine at the time of its manufacture, according to the specifications of the purchaser, but it cannot be adjusted to fluctuate depending on the day of the week or the time of day.

Here's another one you might hear. It goes like this: The trick to finding a loose slot machine is to take its temperature. The warm ones are the loose ones. Again, this is a rule that might work in dating but not in casinos. People who believe this go around placing the palms of their hands like religious healers on the slot machines to find the warm ones.

One thing to keep in mind: The looseness or tightness of a slot machine is determined by the return it gives over the long run. The return rate is probably never measured in increments of less than one week. This rate may have nothing to do with the return rate you get during the relatively short time you're playing the machine. The world's tightest machine pays off sometimes, and if it happens to do so on your coin, you aren't going to care about how much was lost by the players before you, or those who will play after you.

A lot of slots players seem to think that the casinos are spending all their time trying to figure out how to trick them into losing their money in slot machines, turning magical dials that tighten machines during the daytime and things like that.

The truth is that the casinos don't have to trick anyone into losing money. The trick is that never, ever does a slot machine pay out more than it takes in over the long run, so the casinos are guaranteed of making money. No tricks involved.

There are those who will tell you that a machine that starts to spit out warm coins is going to pay off a jackpot soon. 'Tain't necessarily so. In fact, there's no relationship whatsoever between the temperature of the coins and the payoff cycle.

CHAPTER SIX
GIMMICKS

Preceding a recent trip to Atlantic City with my old friend
Curtis "Commander Slots" Kentner, there had been advertisements running in northeastern newspapers bragging
about the brand-new Addams Family nickel video slots
available at all Trump casinos.

The Addams Family, of course, was not new, but the machines were, and though Curt and I failed to find the con-
nection between twisted Goth humor and games of chance,
we arrived on the boardwalk to find those machines packed
with players all weekend. We never got a chance to take a
crack at them.

We could have come back at six in the morning and gotten a seat, but by that time we'd moved on. In fact, within a
few steps we felt as if we'd traveled 2,000 miles from the

edge of the Atlantic Ocean to the land of tumbleweeds in Coyote Kate's Slot Parlor.

Since just about every slot machine functions in approximately the same way, casinos allow players to distinguish between them by giving each machine a theme.

The themes aren't always as much fun as the Addams Family—three Uncle Festers with a lit lightbulb in his mouth and you're a jackpot winner!

The Addams Family isn't the only television show to be adapted into a slot machine, of course, although it's sometimes difficult to figure out why anyone chose the shows they did. *Jeopardy!* and *I Dream of Jeannie* are also popular themes for slot machines. Still, as with pinball machines and arcade video games, the theme of the slot machine is what differentiates it from its competition.

ELVIS

I've known people who wouldn't play a slot machine unless it had a picture of Elvis on it. Luckily, at least in Las Vegas, finding a slot machine with a picture of Elvis on it isn't that hard. It's almost always a picture of Elvis singing; the words GOOD LUCK appear nearby as if those were the lyrics. If the Elvis fans couldn't find the machine they wanted, they carried around a little picture of Elvis and taped it on there before inserting their first coin.

COWBOYS AND COWGIRLS

For some reason I have always preferred western themes on the slot machines I play. Perhaps it's because I first fell in

EXER·SLOTS

Now, I'm naturally in fantastic shape. When I feel my aerobic stamina slipping a bit, I fix it with cigars and whiskey. But not everybody is so lucky. Some folks have to—shudder—exercise to stay in shape. Worse, some folks have to exercise every day. This latter group even includes people who love to play slot machines for hours on end.

I used to think that playing slots was plenty of exercise. After all, unless you're the sort who presses the button rather than pulling the handle, your right arm gets plenty of exercise while playing slots. But then I realized that, since there's no such thing as a left-handed slot machine—I don't know why—long-term players are apt to get out of balance, with a right arm that looks like Popeye's and a left arm more reminiscent of Olive Oyl.

What to do? You're playing a hot slot and it's time to go to the gym. Well, for every dilemma there is a bright answer, and in this case it's the Pedal 'n' Play cycle and the Money Mill treadmill. In other words, you don't have to go to the gym—the gym comes to you. These machines are a slot machine/exercise cycle and a slot machine/treadmill, respectively, built into one. Both were big hits at the 2001 World Gaming Congress and Exposition in Las Vegas.

What's to keep the goof-off slots player from getting on one of these machines and playing the game without doing the work? Plenty. The machines are wired so that you can't pull the handle unless you're pedaling the bike or walking the treadmill.

The Flamingo Hilton in Kansas City, Missouri, was among the first to feature the exercise/gambling machines, while other hotels are making plans to add them to their spas or create specific exercise areas within their casinos. Recognizing that motivation is the key to any successful exercise program, slot machines and exercise machines appear to be a perfect match. In fact, this may just be the beginning. How about a roulette wheel that won't go around unless everyone at the table is pedaling his or her brains out? Or a Wayne Newton show in which Wayne won't sing unless everyone in the audience is doing jumping jacks?

The possibilities are endless.

love with slots in Reno, where a guy in a cowboy hat isn't necessarily from out of town.

And maybe that's why I'm fond of the new Wild, Wild West Casino at Bally's Park Place on the boardwalk in Atlantic City—which is just a hop, skip, and a jump from the crowded Addams Family bank at Trump Plaza.

The Wild, Wild West Casino is inside an old western town facsimile, quaint amid the daring architecture of Atlantic City. And in this casino is a piece of slot machine heaven known as Coyote Kate's Slot Parlor.

Running a casino involves knowledge of psychology as much as it demands knowledge of business. And Bally's—which, after all, manufactures slot machines—has taken the differentiation of its slots a step farther.

It personified them.

You see, Bally's hired a beautiful actress to play Coyote Kate, and she occasionally makes public appearances at her Slot Parlor, with cowgirl hat, kerchief round her neck, shirt tied up for a bare midriff, and dungarees that have been spray-painted on.

If you go to Coyote Kate's to play the slots, you might run into Kate—or you just might be treated to a free show by the Dance Ranch Country Line Dancers. Sure, it's cornier than all get-out, but folks in Atlantic City don't necessarily want Shakespeare—and it's a change from the constant near-deafening sound of thousands of simultaneously spinning slots.

Oh, and I almost forgot to tell you the best thing about Kate's Slot Parlor: The machines there guarantee a 97 percent return. Yikes!

Do not walk there. Run.

CHAPTER SEVEN
DOING THE MATH

In the old days, to figure the odds of getting a particular combination on a single play, you squared the number of symbols on each reel—that is, you multiplied it by itself—as many times as there were reels. In other words, if you had three reels with 15 symbols each, and there's one cherry on each reel, the odds of getting three cherries would be 1 in 15 × 15 × 15, or 1 in 3,375.

People didn't know how good they had it. Up until the mid-1930s, the worst years of the Great Depression, most reels on slot machines had only 10 symbols on them. There were exactly 1,000 possible combinations. The casinos were suckers.

In contrast, there are four-reel computer slots today with 128 images on each of four reels, meaning that there are 262,144,000 possible combinations. Quite a difference. That's an extreme example, but still, the modern slot machine has more than 30,000 possible combinations.

Here's how you figure out the odds of one particular combination coming up. If you have three reels and there are 20 symbols on each reel (the same 20 on each reel), you multiply 20 × 20 × 20 to find that there are 8,000 different combinations—and only 20 of them are three of a kind.

The casinos exponentially increased their advantage when reels began to stop between symbols. Now many machines have reels with, say, 20 symbols, but 40 different stopping positions, since the space between the symbols also counts.

This means that the chances of getting three of a kind decrease dramatically. Now you multiply 40 × 40 × 40 to get a whopping 64,000 different combinations—and only 15 of them are three of a kind.

Now, don't get too discouraged. When you read that a modern computerized slot machine has 262,144,000 possible combos, you're apt to feel like winning a jackpot is about as remote as winning a national lottery. But it's not that bad.

That's because the machine is computerized. All of those combinations do not have to stop at all of the combinations of positions the same number of times. It's the percentage of payout that you're interested in—the number of coins the machine regurgitates for every 100 coins it eats.

HOW PAYOUT RATE WORKS

To see how this works, let's take a look at a very simple early slot machine, one with three reels and 10 symbols on each reel. The first two reels are identical. Each has five horseshoes, two spades, one diamond, one heart, and a bell. The third reel is different. It has two stars, two spades, three diamonds, one heart, and two bells.

The machine's most frequent payout is for two horseshoes with something other than a star on the third reel, which pays out two coins when it occurs and should occur 200 times for every 1,000 plays. We pick 1,000 plays because there are 1,000 possible combinations on the three reels (10 × 10 × 10).

That 200 figure comes from 5 (the number of times the horseshoe appears on the first reel) times 5 (the number of times the horseshoe appears on the second reel) times 8. The 8, in turn, comes from the 10 spots on the third reel minus the 2 bells, which, as we shall see, pay more.

So over the course of 1,000 plays, the machine pays out 400 coins because just two horseshoes come up. If that third reel does come up a star, the machine pays off four coins. Out of 1,000 plays, the combination of two horseshoes and a star is expected to come up 50 times (5 × 5 × 2; the 2 represents the 10 posi-

tions on the third reel minus the 8 positions that don't have bells on them) for a total payoff of 200 coins.

For you math buffs, this means that two horseshoes should come up a total of 250 times, 50 of them with a star and 200 of them with something else on the third reel.

When three spades come up, the machine pays off eight coins. Three spades can be expected to come up eight times out of every 1,000 plays. That's the two times it appears on each reel multiplied by itself three times. So for three spades, the machine pays out 64 coins per 1,000 plays.

For three diamonds the machine pays off 12 coins. This combination is expected to come up three times per 1,000 plays for a total payoff of 36 coins. Three hearts pays 16 coins and is expected to come up once per 1,000 plays—there's one bell on each reel, so one is multiplied by itself three times—for a total payoff of 16 coins.

The most generous payout in the machine is for three bells, which pays 20 coins each time it happens. Since there are two bells on the third reel, along with one apiece on the first two reels, three bells can be expected to occur twice as often as three hearts. The combination can be expected to occur twice per 1,000 plays for a total payout over that period of 40 coins.

Adding up all the payouts, you find that this simple three-reel machine with 10 symbols on each reel pays out only 756 coins for every 1,000 it consumes. That's a payout rate of 75.6 percent—not very good for the player.

By the mid-1930s machines were already a good deal more complex—but the odds for the player were no better. In fact, they had grown a little worse.

The Mills machines made during the peak of the depression had 20 symbols on each of three reels for (20 × 20 × 20) 8,000 possible combinations. For every 8,000 plays, the machine paid out 6,010 coins. That's a payout rate of 75.1 percent.

By the mid-1970s the odds for the player had improved a great deal. Let's take a look at a 1975 Bally machine that had 22 symbols on each of three reels.

This meant that the machine had 10,648 possible combinations. But over the course of these plays the machine paid out 10,062 coins, for a nifty payout rate of 94.5 percent.

I'll spare you the math on the more complicated modern machines. But here's the bottom line: A machine with three reels and 32 stops per reel that can be played with either one coin or two coins per play has a total number of possible combinations of 32,768. But—and this is key—when it's played two coins at a time, it pays out 31,231 coins for each 32,768 played, for a payout rate of 95.3 percent. When it's played one coin at a time, it pays out only 30,431 coins for each 32,768 plays, for a payout rate of 92.9 percent. So for those of you who might think that the one-coin bet is automatically more conservative than the two-coin bet, take heed. Over the long haul, the two-coin bettor is going to do better.

As you can see, the number of possible combinations on the reels and the payout rate are not connected. It might seem that a simple old machine with only 10 symbols on a reel would be bound to pay off better than a modern machine with 22 possible stopping positions on each reel—but in reality the opposite is true.

It's not the number of combinations that matters. It's the rules by which the machine plays that matter.

That's why it's so important to read your machine before you start playing it. You'd be surprised how many rip-off machines get played all the time, despite the fact that they display, in clear, easy-to-read type, just how they're going to rip you off.

CHAPTER EIGHT
COMPUTER GAMES

The modern computerized slot machine contains a computer chip. This chip continually generates random combinations of numbers. In some cases the chip will generate as many as 16 billion possible combinations before it will have to repeat itself.

The number of possible combinations approaches infinity in all practical applications. The random number determines which symbols will appear when each of the reels stops "spinning." The spinning, of course, is mere computer animation on a video screen.

There are no real reels.

The computer is doing all of this in minute fractions of a second. A nanosecond after the computer chooses the random number that determines which symbols appear, it looks up this outcome on a chart to see if it keeps your coin or pays out.

FORGET YOUR OLD MATH

When you're dealing with a computerized slot machine, you can no longer figure out your average payback by taking the payoff table and frequency of each symbol on each reel and doing the math. If a three-reel mechanical slot machine has 20 symbols on each reel, 1 of which is a star, then the odds of hitting 3 gold stars would be 1 in 20 × 20 × 20 or 1 in 8,000. We assume that each reel will stop on any symbol with equal probability. Just as would be the case if we replaced a real roulette wheel with a computerized one, the assumption that each result has an equal chance of occurring is no longer true. Consider a computerized slot machine that has, say, three reels with 22 stops on each reel. If each stop on each reel were equally likely to come up, and only one combination qualified for the jackpot, then the odds of hitting the jackpot would be 1 in 22 × 22 × 22 or 1 in 10,648. To see why this isn't true when a computer chip is in charge, let's look at the Quartermania machine as an example. Let's say that this machine, with a progressive jackpot, offers a jackpot of $1,421,399 on September 1, 2001. If a player hits the jackpot with, on the average, 1 out of every 10,648 quarters he plays, then the machine would pay off for every $2,662 it received. It would be very difficult for casinos to stay in business for very long if this were true.

Every second, an IGT, Bally's, or Anchor computerized slot machine (whether or not it's being played) chooses numerous random integers between 1 and 4,294,967,295.

When a player inserts a coin or spins the reels, the machine selects the next three of these random numbers. Each random number is then divided by a specific number—64 or greater in the IGT machines, and 32 for the Bally's. If the divisor were 64, then the remainders would be uniformly distributed integers in the range of 0 to 63. Each of these remainders is then associated or mapped to one of the (usually) 22 stops on the actual reel, one remainder for each reel. These mapping functions are known as "virtual reels" because they're like a 64-position reel but don't physically exist. There is no longer a one-to-one relationship between remainders and positions on the reel. Many remainders are typically mapped to the blank positions directly above or below jackpot symbols; only one remainder will be mapped to the jackpot symbol itself. (Therefore, despite the fact that the jackpot is won infrequently, a player "comes close" to winning regularly.) The manufacturer designs these mapping functions to achieve desired payback percentages requested by the casino. For machines with very large jackpots relative to the coinage, the divisor is much greater—for example, it's 256 or 512 for games like Quartermania and Megabucks—to achieve very long odds of hitting the jackpot. Assuming 1 number out of 256 were mapped to each jackpot symbol, the odds of hitting the jackpot would be in 1 in 16,777,216.

The computerized slot machine manufacturer known as IGT owns the patent on the process described above and has allowed Bally's a license—but stipulating that the divisor can't be greater than 32, thus not allowing Bally's to create machines with huge jackpots and small coinages. IGT leases the use of its idea to many other makers of slot machines.

As we've seen, one of the major differences between a computerized slot machine and a mechanical one is that, with the mechanical reels, all of the symbols on a reel had an equal probability of coming up. After 1,000 spins, each of the symbols on each reel should have come up about the same number of times. If a slot builder wanted one symbol to come up more often than others, it was simply put on the reel twice.

But this was clumsy. The builder could only make the symbol come up twice as often. The new computerized machines can be programmed so that one symbol comes up more frequently than another, and at *any* percentage of difference.

Cherries can come up on the left reel 14 percent more frequently than oranges, which in turn come up 3 percent more frequently than plums. In other words, 3 percent more of the random numbers being chosen by the computer chip told the left reel to come up oranges than plums, and 14 percent more of these random numbers told the left reel to come up cherries than oranges. So the computer chip, by taking physical reality out of the game, greatly enhances the variety of games and payouts that can be offered—but it does nothing for the predictability of those outcomes.

Just as was the case with mechanical slots, under the law computerized machines must be programmed by the manufacturer—although this can be done to the specifications of the casino—and then left alone after that.

CHANGING CHIPS

On the boardwalk, for example, casinos are not allowed to routinely change the computer chip inside a machine. If they want to change a chip, they have to notify the gaming regulators. A specialist from the Division of Gaming Enforcement will then come to the casino and observe while the computer chip is changed.

The regulations for changing computer chips are not as stringent out in the desert, but they still make the job painful for the casinos by requiring a plethora of paperwork. There's also a regulation stating that a new chip can only be inserted after it has been approved by Nevada regulators.

This is something to keep in mind when the player on the next machine over tries to tell you that the machines are looser on weekends and tighter on weekdays. The truth is that, if we assume that all the casinos are playing by the rules, the machines haven't a clue what day of the week it is, or what time of the day.

The machines *are* allowed to have mechanisms that keep track of which player is on the machine—a credit system using the Slots Player Card noted in chapter 3. This mechanism can be attached to a clock and a calendar. Connecting the clock and calendar to the computer chip determining payoffs would be illegal, however.

The big casinos probably don't spend a lot of time deciding what specifications they want to put into their computer chips. The truth is that the manufacturers offer several standard packages and, since the casinos usually—make that almost always—buy more than one machine at a time, it's not unusual for several or many machines to show up at once, all of which will pay off at a steady and near-identical rate over the long haul.

CHAPTER NINE
MONEY MANAGEMENT

THINGS TO DETERMINE BEFORE YOU START

1. Decide beforehand how much money you're willing to lose.
2. Decide how many times you want to play in the casino. (How long is your trip?)
3. Divide the amount of money by the number of times you want to play to determine the maximum amount you're willing to lose for each session. **Never lose more than this per session! Walk away!**

KNOW WHERE YOU ARE

While you're actually playing, it's important that you know where you stand financially. For this reason I suggest feeding the machine with paper money; it will then record your contributions and earnings on a digital display. You'll know exactly how many credits—that is, coins—you are up or down at any given time. That's a better way to keep track of your money than looking into your bucket and trying to figure out if the level of coins is up or down.

BEWARE OF SKILL BUTTONS

Avoid like the plague any machine that features something called a "skill button." These buttons supposedly allow players to speed up or slow down the reels, which would let them use their "skill" to increase their chances of winning the jackpot.

Skill buttons are illegal. The ones that do exist don't work. In fact, skill buttons usually aren't attached to anything. They are a pure unadulterated rip-off.

THIRSTY PLAYERS PAY HEED

Those of you who are casino veterans know that you can't sit in at the craps table or the roulette wheels or the blackjack table for very long before a beautiful waitress offers you a complimentary drink. That's because these are considered "thinking" games, so the casino is going to do everything it can to alter your ability to think. Thus, the free alcohol.

Go into a major casino and play the slots and you could be at one machine for days before a casino employee will notice. Wait for a free drink and you'll die of thirst.

If you want to play the slot machines yet be catered to as if you were a blackjack player, you have to go to some of the smaller slots parlors, perhaps in Reno or downtown Las Vegas.

In the smaller establishments, a greater percentage of the income comes from slots players, so the slots players are treated more nicely. Even so, don't count on champagne. Beer and house liquor is about the best you can hope for.

PSYCHOLOGICAL BARRIERS TO QUITTING WHILE AHEAD

Be aware that, psychologically, casinos want nothing more than for us to play away our winnings. Winning is so much fun that, having won, we almost always want to do nothing more than win again.

"There's only one rule to winning at the slot machines," says regular player Rita Benson. "Quit while you're ahead."

Say you're playing a quarter machine. The modern slot machine will accept $20 bills and automatically allow you to play that amount by transforming the cash into credits— in this case 80 credits.

However, if you hit for, say, $100 on your first pull of the arm, you can't press a button and get five $20 bills. The machine will transform your winnings into fresh credits so that the easiest thing to do is continue playing.

If you want to cash out at this point—quit while you're ahead, in other words—you have to take the money in quarters. This means that before you can walk out of the casino with your profit in your pocket, you have to wait in line with your bucket of coins and have the "silver" turned into paper.

Now, if you're going to play a progressive machine and are an all-or-nothing type of player, you have a choice to make before you ever put the first coin in the slot.

You have to determine just how much you're willing to lose. Without frequent small payoffs to keep you close to even, you will immediately fall behind on one of these machines, and you'll get deeper and deeper into the hole until—well, until you either hit the jackpot or quit. Know how much you are in the red and, when you reach the magic number, quit. Promptly. Without even giving it a thought.

I shouldn't have to tell you this, because it's simply a matter of common sense, but pay heed nonetheless. Every year people do fall into this trap.

Don't play slot machines because you think it's going to soothe some sort of pain you have. Don't go to Vegas or Atlantic City because you just broke up with your boyfriend or girlfriend.

Playing slot machines should be fun, not therapy. Players who insist on using slot machines as their therapy quickly empty their pockets and end up sleeping under the boardwalk rather than in one of those luxury hotels.

CHAPTER TEN
CHEATING

Is it possible to cheat at a slot machine? Of course. The most common form of cheating is known as "claiming," whereby a player contacts a casino employee and says that her machine hit but her payout either didn't come at all or, when it did come, it was short.

With today's modern slot machines a casino employee can usually tell if the player is telling the truth, so unless there's a tremendous amount of money involved, the player is given the benefit of the doubt. And today's modern casinos are under constant and thorough camera surveillance. Cheaters can not only be found but also be easily convicted in court.

Some cheaters have been known to stand around and watch until a player hits the jackpot. If this player gathers up the coins and leaves without playing the machine one more time, the cheater goes to a casino employee and claims that he hit the jackpot but didn't get any money. Once again, this had a chance of working years ago, but today's machines will indicate unerringly whether or not the machine has already paid out.

If you want to make a false claim, then, my advice is— don't. If your machine really did shortchange you, of course, don't hesitate to tell someone. Your problem can usually be verified and remedied without much fuss.

The other common form of cheating is called "slugging." That's where a player uses slugs—metal discs other than U.S. coins or casino tokens—instead of coins. There are slugs that work in slot machines, but the downside is a harsh one. Get caught and you're looking at jail time.

Back in the old days, some cheaters used to get away with gluing a string to a coin. They would insert the coin, pull the arm, and then use the string to pull the coin back out through the slot. By doing this again and again they could play for free for as long as they wanted, or until they got caught. It has been a long time since such a scheme could work. Anticheat devices in modern slot machines make such an act impossible today.

In every community there exists the very bottom of the totem pole, the lowest form of known life, and in the slot machine section of any casino that lowest life-form is called the "silverminer."

Silverminers aren't quite thieves and they aren't quite panhandlers, but they are looked down upon—even by full-fledged cheaters. Silverminers are people who don't play the slots, but rather look in trays just after people leave to see if they can collect a coin or two that has been left behind. There must be a 12-step program somewhere that could help these pathetic people.

SHUTTING DOWN THE SCAMSTERS

One of the biggest confusions players have regarding slot machines themselves is a small warning that sometimes appears on those machines that accept a varying number of coins.

The sign is worded differently depending on where you are, but it reads something to the effect of: MAKE SURE ALL YOUR COINS HAVE REGISTERED BEFORE PULLING THE HANDLE.

Since coins register almost instantly, you really don't have anything to worry about. It would be a rare fluke if you put in a coin and it didn't count.

So why is the sign there? To ward off potential cheaters, that's why. Before the sign appeared there was a common scam in which a player who had just hit while playing one coin would squawk to a casino employee that he had actually played three coins and the stupid machine messed up. Now the scamsters have been forewarned and their squawking, instead of bearing fruit, will get only a "Tsk, tsk, tsk, we told you so."

There have been cases, of course, where a slot machine has genuinely malfunctioned after a player inserted a coin. It happens when, say, there's a small piece of bubble gum on the quarter and it won't track properly inside the machine. It's impossible for the machine to hit the jackpot under these circumstances, however. The machine will immediately lock so that the handle can't be pulled. The machine knows that you've inserted a coin and that, for some reason, it can't use it. Either the machine will remain locked until the problem is fixed, or, if it can, the machine will return the coin or coins that have already been inserted and instruct you to start over.

When slot machines break down, it's usually not the coin-taking mechanism that goes but rather the reels with the symbols on them. This makes sense, if you think about it, because these are the parts that move the most. When a machine goes out of order it's often because one of its reels isn't spinning at the same speed as the others, or has stopped spinning completely. If this happens to a machine that you're playing, stop immediately and contact a casino employee. The casino has a legal obligation to take any slot machine that's out of order out of service immediately.

CHAPTER ELEVEN
PROFILES OF SLOT
MACHINE WINNERS

What follows are the true-life stories of a few individuals who have used strategy to increase their chances of winning at the slots. Some of them follow personal rules regarding how they choose which machine to play on, as well as how long they play on it. Some have changed their luck for the better by switching casinos. They did their homework and found out which casinos offer the loosest slots. Others have increased their casino profits by taking advantage of freebies, comps, and the other benefits available out there. Still others have altered their money-management techniques to turn things for the better.

So here are the stories of the winners, and from each there is (at least) one lesson to be learned.

CASE HISTORY I: THE MEANINGLESSNESS OF LONG-TERM PAYBACK RATES IN A SHORT-TERM WORLD

BETTIE B.

A retired writer of children's books, Bettie lives in Jacksonville, Florida, and is a frequent visitor to the casinos along the Gulf Coast. Her initial misunderstanding when it came to slot machines was a common one: She thought that her chances of going home a winner were automatically enhanced with a higher promised payback rate. That is, she figured that if she always played on a machine that guaranteed a 97 percent payback, her chances of going home a winner were automatically better than if she played on a machine that guaranteed only a 90 percent payback.

"My problem was that I overestimated the frequency with which the machines had to be accountable to their own guarantees," Bettie says. "And as it turns out, that isn't very frequent at all."

What Bettie was doing was concentrating her strategy on payback rate and ignoring a second factor known as payback schedule.

There are jackpot machines, for example, that guarantee a 95 percent payback. But the jackpot might be $950,000. This means that 100,000 players, all playing $10 apiece in this machine, would have to lose every single time before, on the average, one player would win the $950,000. The machine took in $1 million and gave out $950,000, so its payback rate was 95 percent, just like it said it was. But for any of those players who put $10 into the machine, the chances of going home a winner were no better than 1 in

100,000. If you played $100 on this machine, you could improve your chances of winning to 1 in 10,000. If you were willing to play $1,000, your odds of winning would be down to a can't-lose 1 in 1,000. You get the idea.

Of course, this is a slight exaggeration. Even the biggest megabuck progressive jackpot machines give smaller paybacks every once in a while to keep the player interested. But the chances of winning more than you lose on such a machine without winning the jackpot are pretty slim.

On the other hand, a machine that gives back $9 for every $10 it takes has a payback rate of only 90 percent—5 percent less than the machine in our previous example. But this 90 percent payback machine might make winners out of 45 percent of the players who play it, so that your chances of making money on it during any short stint of play are only slightly worse than even-up.

"I spent hours playing slots that guaranteed great payback rates, and I was going broke," Bettie says. "I would spend hour after hour on icy machines, wondering when my luck was going to turn. And—this is the most important part—I wouldn't move to a new machine after being down so much money, because I believed that I could get 97 percent of it back, or whatever was the guarantee of the machine, if I only played for long enough."

What Bettie didn't realize was that there are some machines that only a millionaire could play for long enough to guarantee receiving the guaranteed payback. And by that time the odds are that he'd be down $50,000.

"Now I stick to the machines that have a modest jackpot but pay back more regularly. I still lose every now and again, but I swear I have been winning more than losing ever since I smartened up and revised my strategy," Betty proclaims.

There is a middle ground between the two extremes: You can find machines with smaller progressive jackpots attached to larger banks of machines. On these machines a smaller percentage of each coin played is put into the jackpot. Therefore, there's more money to pay back to each player. So these machines offer the excitement of possibly winning a big jackpot, without making you feel like an automatic loser if that jackpot doesn't end up in your hands.

CASE HISTORY II: THE POPULAR SLOT PARLOR IS PROBABLY THE LOOSEST

CONSTANCE R.

Constance R. is a 66-year-old widow from Kansas City, Missouri, who loves to play the casinos in her area and travels to Las Vegas four times a year to, as she puts it, "see the lights and hear the stars."

Years ago, Constance rarely won when she played the slot machines.

"My husband would head straight for the sports book, and I'd play the slots. He usually won and I usually lost. It was only after he passed away that I learned an important lesson about slot machines: Not all casinos are the same— and the casino with the best sports book is not always the casino with the best slot machines," Constance says. "I learned to do what I call window-shop."

Constance now goes from casino to casino before she even drops her first coin. She's on a scouting mission.

"I find out which slot parlors are crowded and which are empty," she says. "If there are no other players in a certain section of slot machines, or in a certain casino, then there's usually a pretty good reason why," she says. "It's the same as when you're driving down the road looking for a place to eat. There are two truck stops. One is packed and the trucks have filled up the parking lot. The other one is practically deserted. Which one do you think has the better food?"

Constance has learned over the years that slots players are not like Greta Garbo. They never "vant to be alone."

This advice goes out with particular fervor to those who choose their hotel/casino by which stars are performing there during their stay. They feel that they "owe" it to the hotel where they're registered to lose money in its casino. Unless you're in a casino that has no nearby competition, don't be afraid to "window-shop." A casino might have the Beatles and the Rolling Stones playing a double bill in its arena, but that doesn't mean its slots parlor is loose.

CASE HISTORY III: PLAY IN VEGAS

KENNY G.

Kenny G. is not a jazz musician. His name just sounds that way. This Kenny is actually a 43-year-old schoolteacher from Newark, New Jersey. He wasn't always a school-teacher. He started out as an up-and-comer in the garment industry, but he burned out and/or had a midlife crisis about seven years ago. He quit his job in the factory, went back to school, and reemerged as a math teacher. Oddly, Kenny's career at the slot machines has followed a similar course.

"I used to lose almost every time I went to the casino. Since I'm a New Jersey boy, I naturally favored the casinos of Atlantic City over those out in Las Vegas. They were just so much more convenient," says Kenny. "Then I wised up."

What happened?

"I read two reports, one from Atlantic City and one from Las Vegas, and I was shocked to discover that the payback percentages in Las Vegas were so much better than those in Atlantic City that the casinos on the boardwalk no longer seemed so convenient to me," Kenny says.

The reports Kenny is referring to were from, respectively, the New Jersey Casino Control Commission and the Nevada State Gaming Control Board. The numbers showed that there was a 3 to 6 percent difference between the average paybacks in the two gambling towns.

(For you high rollers who are already booking first-class flights to Las Vegas upon hearing this, it should be noted that the advantage Las Vegas has over Atlantic City holds true for only small-denomination machines. Once you get to the $5-and-up machines the Vegas advantage disappears.)

Of course, now that he has his summers off, Kenny can go out to the desert to play two months out of the year.

CASE HISTORY IV: GETTING THE MOST OUT OF THE CASINO COMP SYSTEM

SETH L.

Seth L. is a 57-year-old grocery store owner from Brooklyn, New York. He switched from the L column to the W column when it came to playing the slots after he learned to take advantage of the casinos' comp practices.

"The process was slow. I went from being a guy who paid full price for everything to a guy who gets most of my stuff for free one step at a time. I had heard people talking about comps, but I always thought you had to lose a lot of money at the tables to get complimentary stuff from the casinos or from their attached hotels.

"I started out by signing up for everything I could, whether it be a credit-card application with a comp (I'd cancel the credit card as soon as I could), or a newspaper advertisement that included some sort of coupon.

"I got the card that you actually insert into the slot machines. It measures how much you play, and that way you earn comps. But the real quantum leap in my ability to get complimentary stuff came when I joined a slot machine club.

"I found that, after paying my entrance fee, the club made life around the casino much easier in many different ways. Just last weekend I went to a casino with my club. They had a scheduled event for us, with tournaments and free playing as well. There was a room of slot machines set aside that was just for our club. The machines were promised to be the loosest anywhere in New Jersey or Connecticut. I heard a rumor that, for the club events, they bring in machines that have a 99-plus percent payback rate. I wouldn't have thought such a thing was possible. But out of the 75 people in the club at the event, I would estimate that 60 or so were winners, even after playing many hours, sometimes on the same machine. And the remaining 15, who actually lost money at the machines, didn't lose very much.

"Okay, so the casinos rig the machines to be nice to club members. That's pretty cool, but the most amazing thing is the amount of other stuff you get for free," says Seth.

Here's a list of comps that Seth received during one weekend club event at a major casino:

- Free hotel room
- Free buffet twice a day—all you can eat
- A free show with complimentary drinks
- Complimentary drinks while playing the slots
- A goody bag containing casino souvenirs, dice, a canvas bag, a deck of cards, a T-shirt, and more.

So if you really want to be a winner at the slots, join a slot club and, like Seth, take full advantage of the casino's comp system.

CASE HISTORY V: PLAY THE MACHINES THAT TAKE THE LARGEST COINS

CYNTHIA D.

Cynthia D., or Cindy as she prefers to be called, is a 27-year-old fashion photographer who has an apartment in Los Angeles but travels much of the time. Cindy likes to work near a casino, because she uses the slot machines to un-wind. She improved her luck at the slot machines by chang-ing the denomination she played in.

"I used to play nickel slots and maybe, every once in a while, if I was feeling daring, the quarter slots. It wasn't so much that I was afraid to lose," she says, shyly admitting that financially she has done okay for herself, despite her under-30 status. "It was just that I saw losing as an inevitability and I figured that, the smaller the coin I was playing, the more I would get to play before I lost whatever amount I had allotted for myself," Cindy says.

Every once in a while Cindy would win, but much of the time, like a self-fulfilling prophecy, Cindy would merely play until her nickels ran out. Then she'd call it a night.

"Then someone told me that you have a better chance of making money at the slot machines if you play the really expensive ones," Cindy said. "It took some courage, but I started playing the $5 machines. I take my time and play slowly, I enjoy the better class of people that I am surrounded by, and I've found that my luck at the slots has been much improved since I made the move."

Is there a mathematical reason for Cindy's change of luck? You bet. The casinos want you to risk as much of your money as they can seduce out of you, so they're going to discourage you from playing the nickel machines and encourage you to play the $5 machines. It's the same concept as that behind "You have to play the machine for the maximum number of coins to have any chance of winning the jackpot."

According to figures (five years old, but they've stayed about the same) provided by the Nevada State Gaming Control Board, the average payback percentage on a nickel machine along the strip is 92. They move up to 92.5 percent for dime machines, and leaps to 95 percent for quarter slots. Fifty-cent slots and dollar slots each had an average return of 95.5 percent. Five-dollar slots returned 96.5 percent, and the $25 slots returned 97 percent. (Quick: Whose face is on the $25 bill?)

Las Vegas has slot machines that will take $500 off your credit card with each pull of the arm. There have been no studies of the return rates for these, but you can assume that it is, on the average, between 97 and 99 percent.

The reason is that the players who use the highest-denomination machines are much more apt to grumble and make a fuss (or—shudder—take their business elsewhere) if they lose. Thus the game is made increasingly fair for them. Those who play the nickel slots all too often have the same mentality that Cindy had when she played them—to simply play until the nickels run out.

And this the-bigger-the-denomination-the-bigger-the-payback-percentage rule isn't true just in Las Vegas. It applies whether you're playing on a riverboat or in Monte Carlo. So if you can afford it, play the larger-denomination machines. It worked for Cindy, and it can work for you.

Do not take this to mean that every quarter machine has a lower payback rate than every dollar machine. We are, as always, talking *average* and *over the long haul.* There are tight dollar machines and there are loose quarter machines.

If you're uncomfortable playing the more expensive machines, then don't do it. If you're a nickel guy or gal, then you should play the nickel slots. Simply search for the loosest among the slot machines that takes the coin you most like to play. The idea here is not to be miserable with worry while you wait for your ship to come in.

A psychological approach like that is bound to influence your decision making in the worst way. Besides, if you're not having fun at the slot machines, do something else.

Any other benefits to playing the big-money slots?

"You bet," Cindy says. "It's a heck of a lot easier to get a free drink!"

CASE HISTORY VI: BE PROUD OF YOUR LOVE OF SLOTS

ROBERT F.

Robert F.'s lesson is a simple one: Don't be shy. You play slots. You love slots. You live and breathe slots. Slots are your old lady, or your old man. Say it loud: You are a slots player and you are proud.

Robert is a 37-year-old insurance adjuster who, as a younger man, felt that playing the slots was somehow embarrassing.

"I was menaced by stereotypes, I guess," Robert says. "I felt like I would be at the poker table or playing blackjack or the ponies if I were a real man."

It's a sad story, no doubt about it, but it gets sadder. Because Robert was so shy about his slots playing, he did tremendous damage to his chances of being a winner.

"I used to seek out the darkest, quietest corners of the casino, and I always played early in the morning, between four and seven o'clock, when I knew I could find whole banks of machines that were vacated. Have you ever been in a casino that's so empty that it approaches quiet? It's creepy," Robert says.

Since a portion of the psychology behind how casinos design their parlors is to make sure that winners are seen and heard while losers go quietly away without being noticed, Robert was playing into the house's hands because of his shyness.

Well, this sad story has a happy ending.

"I realized how silly I was being about my embarrassment. I went to casinos during the busiest hours and went to the busiest banks of slots, and I was amazed by what I saw. There were almost half who were men, and not just retired guys either—plenty of guys my age and younger, too. I saw—for the first time, I think—that playing the slots is the hip thing that it is."

CASE HISTORY VII: HOW TO FIND THE LOOSE SLOTS

BRIAN D.

Brian D., a 32-year-old native of Las Vegas, is married with three kids. To make ends meet, he is working two jobs, one of them at night at one of the major casinos. Because of his busy schedule—and the fact that he would like to see his wife and kids every once in a while—Brian can't gamble whenever he wants to.

"Even though I work in a casino," Brian says, "I don't get to gamble there whenever I like. I'm not allowed to gamble when I'm working, obviously, and when I'm not working I have to be at my other job. Since I like to be at home when the kids wake up in the morning, the only time I get to play the slots is at four and five in the morning, when there are the least number of people in the slot parlor. I know they say that Vegas never sleeps, but it definitely gets drowsy in the hours just before dawn. So I'm there when the place is the least crowded."

Because of this, Brian says, it's more difficult to determine where the loose slots are.

"In my own casino, when I'm working but on break, I scout out the banks of machines and try to get a feel for what's hot and what's not—but it's hard without being able to observe for any length of time."

So how do you tell the loose ones from the tight ones?

"I watch the veterans. There aren't as many slots players tugging away at that hour, but some of them are wise and cagey, and they know what they're doing. I keep an eye on them. If I see a cluster of players who look like they've done all right by the slots over the years, then I camp out near them—although never directly next to them, of course. Everyone knows that the casinos never, ever put two loose machines directly next to each other."

And like all good slots players, Brian knows how to connect the dots.

"If I see a machine hitting for a player again and again one night, and then the next night it seems cold, I hop on that machine as soon as it's available. I know that it's only a matter of time before it gets hot again. Machines don't change from day to day or from hour to hour. They stay the same. Once you've located a hot machine, it stays a hot machine until they recalibrate it or change its computer chip or something."

Be true and faithful to the ones you know are hot, Brian says, because they will be your best friends.

"They're fickle, too," he adds, "because they do go through short stints when they're tight—although those periods are shorter than the hot periods, which is what makes the machine loose in the first place. They're also fickle because they're popular. Chances are, if you know that a machine is loose, there are other slots players smart enough and observant enough to know it also, so it's going to be tougher to get on that machine than any other."

CASE HISTORY VIII: PLAY THE MAXIMUM NUMBER OF COINS ON MULTICOIN MACHINES

MARVIN W.

Marvin W. is a 23-year-old photo technician for a Nevada defense contractor. His story is a common one. He thought that playing a four-coin quarter machine with one quarter per play was the same as playing a one-coin-only quarter machine. Okay, I'll let Marvin explain.

"When you play a quarter machine, you pull the handle, you take your chances," Marvin said. "And I thought it was the same thing when you put a single quarter into a four-quarter machine."

As we have learned, the chances of winning increase on multiple-coin machines when you play more coins, with the maximum chance of winning always coming when you play the maximum number of coins per play.

"I felt kind of dumb when I first learned of my error. In fact, I was horrified when I learned that I had been playing for jackpots using single-coin plays on machines that only offer jackpots when the maximum number of coins is being played."

It gets worse.

"I had even been playing single coins on multicoin machines that had progressive jackpots," Marvin says angrily. "I spent all that time looking at the jackpot numbers go up, up, up—and the whole time I was spending money without even giving myself a chance of winning the big money. It cheeses me off when I think about it. It was like I was throwing my money away."

But as always, our case history has a happy ending. Not long after Marvin smartened up and began to play the maximum number of coins allowed on all multiple-coin machines, he hit the jackpot—and it was a progressive jackpot as well.

"I was looking at the jackpot numbers, which are always in red lights on a screen up above the bank of machines. The number is always going up, up, up. Sometimes it gets very high, and sometimes it's kind of low because somebody recently hit it and the number started over. I put in my four quarters and pulled the handle. I watched the numbers and I was sort of aware that the reels clicked into place just as the number stopped growing and froze at—I'll never forget it—$127,875.14. Then the number started flashing. Then it sounded like there was an air raid and everybody was looking at me. It was the greatest moment of my life."

The lesson, of course, is: Always, always, give yourself the best possible chance of winning, with every pull of the handle.

CASE HISTORY IX: DON'T BE HYPNOTIZED BY THE SIGHTS AND SOUNDS

BRENDA S.

There is no doubt about it: the sights and sounds of a casino can have a hypnotic effect on a player.

This is by design. The casinos don't want you to be able to think clearly. Here's a story about a slots player who had a problem with the hypnotic effect of the ambience, as well as of the machines themselves.

"I never intended to be a stupid slots player, I can assure you of that," says Brenda S.—a 44-year-old bookkeeper from Bend, Oregon—in her own defense. "I would map out a game plan, have my budget in mind, ready to stick to all of my money-management principles, and then boom. I would get in the casino and right away it would start. It was just as if I had taken some kind of drug. The loud ringing noise of all of those slot machines being played at the same time would get me charged up, so that my heart would beat a little bit faster and my adrenaline would start to pump. I don't want to say that I would sweat, but I definitely misted slightly with my excitement."

And that wasn't all.

"I feel like I've had three cups of 100 percent Colombian coffee—and then I start to play the slots. The wheels go around and around and next thing you know I'm starting to feel a little high. Not dizzy, really, but pleasantly relaxed. There's just something soothing about the whole feel of a slot machine handle and watching the reels click to a stop, always one at a time and always in the same order. By now I feel like I've had 100 percent Colombian something else."

Predictably, Brenda's casino high did nothing for her chances of winning.

"I almost always lost," she says sadly. "In fact, the thing that would snap me out of it would be my last coin going into the slot. Knowing that I had to stop playing or dig out more paper money would snap me back into reality. I would find that I had stayed on one machine for far too long, though my game plan always involved moving frequently from machine to machine while observing the behavior of my fellow players. All of that would go down the tubes.

"My problem was that I found the little trance I went into so pleasant that there was a big part of me that didn't want to snap out of it. When the machine I was playing did pay off, I didn't snap out of it at all. I would just go deeper into what I used to call my 'casino-head.'

"But I finally learned that I had to. I had to stay alert. I did this in a couple of ways. Now I wear a Walkman with headphones when I play. I don't listen to a voice saying, 'Stick with your game plan, stick with your game plan,' or anything like that. I listen to good music, but it helps me keep my mind on my strategy. I also have learned to keep my eyes shut for part of the time when the reels are spinning, and that diminishes the spacey feeling. I had to come up with some kind of technique. It was either that or go broke—or give up playing the slots altogether.

"And that's the last thing I want to do."

CASE HISTORY X: ALWAYS PLAY FOR THE BIGGEST JACKPOT

PAUL J.

Paul J. is a 33-year-old ceramics engineer from Bradford, Pennsylvania. Naturally, he goes to Atlantic City to get his slots playing in. He went from being a loser to being a winner when he made a quantum leap in understanding regarding progressive jackpots.

"I learned that when you're playing for a progressive jackpot, and your machine is hooked up to a bunch of other machines, and every machine is contributing to the same jackpot, your chances of winning the jackpot remain the same—fairly slim, if you want to know the truth—no matter how large the jackpot is," says Paul.

"My problem came when I would try to outthink the system. I was convinced that some banks of machines paid out their jackpots more frequently than others, so that the payback rate over the short term was being maintained by machines that paid out their jackpots with relative frequency. This being the case, one or two jackpots would be allowed to go sky high.

"The eventual winners of those humongous jackpots would then get their pictures in the newspapers and be financially set for the rest of their lives, but at the expense of thousands and thousands of gamblers who bet on those machines and lost all their money.

"Now, my thinking was entirely flawed. I was right that the chances of winning a jackpot are almost always prohibitively low, although that didn't stop me—but I'm getting ahead of myself. The flaw was that I believed the chances of winning on a bank of machines with a small progressive jackpot—one that, in other words, had recently been won and had reset—was better than my chances of winning at a bank of machines where the jackpot was huge. I have since learned that the odds of winning the small jackpot and the large jackpot are exactly the same. That being the case, I've made it a point always to play for the progressive jackpot that has grown the largest. If the odds of winning are always the same, then you should always be playing for the largest prize. It's as simple as that. And not long after I made this realization, with the help of a gambling buddy of mine who set me straight, I hit a big progressive jackpot—something that was in seven figures when I got it, and in six after the government took a piece. Still, it was my greatest day ever, and I'm so glad that it didn't happen when I was playing for a relatively puny jackpot."

It should be noted there that there are plenty of slots players out there who believe that their chances of winning the really big progressive jackpots are greater than their chances of winning the smaller jackpots because the big ones are due to be won. These players are also playing under a delusion, but we don't discourage them because they're doing the right thing, even if it's for the wrong reason.

(And I will reiterate: When it comes to any multicoin machine with a jackpot, read the instructions and specifications on the machine closely before you start to play. The chances are good that you have to play the maximum number of coins on every play even to be eligible to win the jackpot.)

CASE HISTORY XI: QUIT THE TIGHT MACHINES QUICKLY

KEITH B.

Even those players whose brains are not prone to great alpha-wave fluctuation can find themselves lingering at a tight machine for too long. Such was the case with Keith B., a 51-year-old jazz musician from Manhattan.

"I had this notion in my head that if a machine was eating up my money, I should stick with it because the machine's nature was bound to change. I figured that I had already suffered through the machine's cold cycle, and the hot cycle was bound to start at any second," Keith says.

Now, this kind of thinking might work if you have preestablished, through observation and research, a machine as a hot machine. Then it might be worthwhile to sit through a dry spell—if you can afford it—because you know that in the long run the machine is a winner. But that's not what Keith was doing.

"I would go for a long weekend down at the boardwalk, walk into a casino, plop myself down at the first machine that was open, and start to crank in the coins. If the machine paid off I would take my money and move on. If it was cold as ice I would stay and stay and stay—and try to warm the machine up. It got to be a very expensive practice," Keith explains.

Another thing Keith would do, often to no avail, was watch a jackpot machine that wasn't paying off.

"I would keep my eye on a player who had been on the same machine for a long time without winning anything. The second that person got up and moved to another machine or cashed in or whatever, I would hop on the machine—the very machine that had proven itself to be a loser. My thinking, of course, was that this machine was due to hit the jackpot. Somehow it never worked, though. I would end up contributing to the jackpot for way too long before the chilling realization would come over me that the same machine that was so cold for the person who played it before me was being just as icy for me."

Then came the day that a little lightbulb went on over Keith's head.

"I realized that I had to stop thinking in terms of cycles," Keith said. "Because every machine's cycle was different, and I had no idea how long a cold cycle would last before a hot one would start. Instead, I thought in terms of hot machines and cold machines in general, as if they were staid, always the same. That isn't precisely true, I realize. But the payback rate of a machine will stay the same throughout its lifetime, unless the casino decides that they want to change it—in which case there's a lot of legal rigmarole they have to go through, so they hardly ever change them. Once I started to think of good machines and bad machines, without trying to gauge the undulating probabilities, my luck improved tremendously. I blow a horn in a small club in Greenwich Village for a living, so I can use all the coins I can get."

CASE HISTORY XII: ALWAYS QUIT WHILE YOU'RE AHEAD

PRUDENCE F.

Prudence F. is a 27-year-old flight attendant for a major commercial airline. Just as Keith in our previous case history was slow to figure out when he had it bad, Prudence was slow to figure out when she had it good.

Prudence's strategy wasn't a bad one. I'll let her tell you:

"I took the advice 'Quit while you're ahead,' to the extreme," explains Prudence. "I wouldn't quit the casino. I would just quit the machine I was playing. My theory was that on every machine you play, there's always a point where you're ahead. When you get to that point, my strategy said, then move on. If you play enough different machines and make a little bit of money at each of them, I figured it would add up by the end of the day."

The flaw in Prudence's plan is twofold:

1. Not every machine is going to offer you a moment when you're ahead, and if the machine doesn't want to offer you such a moment, you can go broke waiting for it to come.

2. Sometimes, if a machine is hot, quitting when you're ahead will do nothing but keep you from getting farther ahead.

The trick, of course, is to tell when that hot machine shifts to cold. The way to avoid playing back your profits is to count the coins you play, between winning plays. If you play that certain number of coins in a row on the machine and you get nothing back, that's a good sign that the machine is cooling off and it's time to move on.

"Not only have I learned not to leave hot machines too quickly, but I've also learned to keep an eye out for other players in my vicinity who leave hot machines too quickly. And when they do, I quickly take their place at that machine. If they don't want to take advantage of the hot machine, I will," says Prudence.

CASE HISTORY XIII: PLAYING TOURNAMENTS

STEVE T.

Steve T. is a 59-year-old college professor at a major northeastern university. He teaches sociology.

"I have tenure at my school, so I no longer have to teach classes during the summer," Steve says. He uses his

CAN LIGHTNING STRIKE TWICE? YOU BET!

If you think that in any given period of time, only one player is going to hit a huge jackpot in any one casino, think again. Sometimes it happens boom, boom, back to back—so that the casino gets thrust into a frenzy of activity over the second hit before it has had a chance to catch its collective breath over the first.

Not long ago there were two jackpot winners within hours of one another in an Indian-owned casino in the Midwest. A 23-year-old housekeeping supervisor and a 64-year-old dairy farmer both hit on what would otherwise have been an uneventful Sunday. Jill Jordan won $1,033,681 playing the Wheel of Fortune slot machine on Sunday afternoon—and a little more than four hours later, bells rang and lights flashed again as Don Karls won $289,624 on the Wheel of Gold slot machine only a few feet away.

Both said they didn't initially realize how much they'd won. For Jill, we can understand her confusion. Two commas in the same number can be a tad boggling for the mind if you're not used to it.

"When I first saw the number," Jill says, "I thought it was $100,000."

The number, of course, was actually $1,033,624.

"Within a few minutes I realized what it was and just kind of shook," says Jill. So what will she be doing with her newfound fortune?

"I'm going to quit my job at Country Inn Suites and become a full-time mom to my four-year-old," she says.

She received $39,757 once the jackpot on the $3-per-play machine was verified Sunday evening. She will get 25 more annual installments in that amount, or can opt for a lump-sum payment. She said she's awaiting details of the lump-sum offer and will then make long-term financial plans.

"I hope to open a photography studio someday," Jill says. "That's been one of my dreams for a long time."

Don Karls said he was planning to sell his cows and retire this fall but will now seek to do so immediately. He got his first of 21 annual payments Sunday for $13,700 and said he will also consider the casino's lump-sum offer when it's made. Don said he hasn't rushed out and bought anything, nor does he have any idea what he'll do with the money long term.

Like Jill, at first glance Don thought he'd won just over $20,000 after playing the 75-cent machine for the 10th time Sunday.

"Then I checked it over and could see it was progressive, that I had won much more," he said.

Okay, now you figure the casino is shot. No more jackpots for a very long time, right? Wrong.

The very next day a 42-year-old, out-of-work Independence, Missouri, man hit a progressive slot machine jackpot at the same casino—and this one was worth more than the first two put together. It was for $2,588,010.

Jonathan Fielding, who was divorced and had fallen "a little behind" on his child-support payments, had been playing the Double Wild Cherry progressive slot since about 8 A.M.—at $10 a pull. Nine and a quarter hours later, at 5:16 P.M., the machine finally hit big.

"I was about ready to go," said the soft-spoken winner, who remained calm among a crowd of players, casino employees, and Gaming Commission agents who crowded around the machine in a party atmosphere. Jonathan received a check for the full amount. The Internal Revenue Service was advised of his winnings, said the casino president. Because of the size of the jackpot, the gambling agent in charge of the casino, according to a press release, "routinely broke several seals on the machine and electronically verified that the game's electronic controls hadn't been tampered with and indeed correctly paid the big jackpot. This whole process tells the public that safeguards are in place against cheating by players or the casino."

Jonathan, who resumed playing after all the excitement died down, said he intended to pay off some bills, take a nice vacation, and set aside some of his winnings for his five-year-old son. The jackpot on that machine reset at $25,000 and started building again with each pull of the handle.

hard-earned time off to indulge in his other passion—the one-armed bandit.

"I love to play slot machine tournaments. I think that playing the tourneys is a lot more exciting than just playing slot machine freelance, if you will. When I just go into a casino and start to play a machine, even after I've done my research to figure out the loose machines from the tight ones, I still feel like it's a battle between me and the machine. Don't get me wrong—I love slot machines. Along with jukeboxes and the electric razor, they're among my favorite machines in the whole, wide world. But a battle between me and a machine—between me and *any* machine—strikes me as a little cold and impersonal. When I play in the slot machine tournaments, it's a battle between me and other thinking human beings. It's me against them, and that's where I find the thrill. I guess that's why it took me so long to figure out what I did about the tournaments.

"You see, I always assumed that all tournaments were the same. It didn't occur to me that I was costing myself a heck of a lot of money just by playing bad tournaments when I could have been playing good ones," Steve says.

What are the things we should look for in a tournament before signing up?

"First thing you need to do is find out how much the prize money is," Steve says urgently. The best tourneys, he notes, will be very proud to talk about the money. They will brag about it. "If the prize money is in small type at the base of the advertisement, forgetaboutit."

Another key factor is how that prize money is distributed. "In some tournaments the winner gets the bulk of the entire purse. In others the winner gets a lesser chunk of the entire bundle, but in those there are better prizes for second and third place, et cetera," Steve explains.

Then there's the matter of the entrance fee. If the prize money is big, sometimes the entrance fee is big as well.

"What you're really looking for is a high ratio between the prize money and the entrance fee," Steve says.

Knowing the rules of the tournament is also very important. "Find out what happens if you run out of coins during the tournament. All contests will provide you with coins to play with at the start of each round, so that you're even-steven with all the other competitors.

"But some tournaments allow players to play with their own coins if they run out during one of the rounds. Some tournaments, on the other hand, will say that any competitor who plays away all of their coins during any round is disqualified and is out of the tournament.

"I like to stay away from the tournaments that let you play with your own money. It seems slightly dishonest, for one thing, since all of a sudden the competitors are no longer playing on a level playing field.

"The player who is willing to subsidize himself—no matter what, just to stay in the contest—is going to have a better chance of winning than the players who aren't willing to endlessly dip into their own resources just to stay in the tournament. Now I know that the people who are subsidizing their own tournament efforts probably aren't going to win anyway, at least not first prize. The winner of every competition, it seems to me, is going to be a person who never runs out of coins, no matter what the rules of the contest are. Still, when you throw in the size of someone's personal pocketbook into the mix, the playing field does tilt.

"I have always suspected that this is how some casinos make the bulk of their money on slot machine tournaments," Steve theorizes. "Casinos are taking advantage of players who get caught up in the speed and the excitement of the tournament. As you know, tournament players play much faster than the freelancers. No one ever uses the handles anymore when they're playing tourneys. The buttons are quicker, and the total number of plays you can get in before the time limit runs out often determines who's the winner at the end. Anyway, players who are bottoming out during an early round are putting more money into the casino—in addition to the entrance fee, which they have already paid— just to avoid ending their day. Even before I realized the wisdom of discriminating among slot machine tournaments, I knew better than to invest in myself at a time like that, especially when my cause was already starting to look like a losing one. Better to cut my losses and try again next time."

Another consideration is: What kinds of perks and comps and various assorted freebies are you going to get from the casino/hotel if you sign up and pay the entrance fee to be in the tournament?

"This is where I really got burned back before I saw the light," says Steve. "I would be playing in a tournament that was buying me free drinks and one buffet lunch when I could have been playing in a tournament that got me a free hotel room, free meals, and free drinks—plus maybe tickets to the fights that night."

So clearly, find out what perks come with your registration. Sometimes this is the most important consideration.

What are the three best ways to find out the details regarding slot machine tournaments in the near future?

Steve says: "One, write or call the casinos that you go to and ask to be put on their mailing list. Two, if you have a computer, e-mail the casinos and ask for information or check on their individual Web sites. And three, join a slot machine tournament club."

CASE HISTORY XIV: KEEPING A RECORD OF YOUR PLAY

JUDITH G.

Judith G. is a 40-something housewife and mother of two. She is married to an accountant. Her problem, when it came to slot machines, was that she would go to the casino with a game plan in mind, but then stray away from that plan as her stint in the slot parlor continued—sometimes as soon as she entered the casino.

"I could never seem to actually do the things that I set out to do. If I was determined to stick with a progressive jackpot in an attempt to make the big bucks, I would end up flitting around the casino playing different machines. It was almost like I would wander aimlessly. On the other hand, if I decided ahead of time that I was going to play a hit-and-run game, trying to make a little something out of each machine I played, I would end up sitting in one place for hours at a machine that most definitely was not making it worth my while."

So how did Judith learn the discipline to stick with her game plan?

"I decided to keep track of every single coin I played. I knew that if I took the time to write something down after every coin I inserted, I wouldn't be as apt to wander and go astray from the strategy. I went out and bought myself an accountant's ledger, with lots of boxes and columns for me to keep my records in."

Judith kept track of the denomination of coin the machine she was playing took, the number of coins she put into each machine, and the number of coins she got back from each.

CASE HISTORY XV: THE HUNT FOR LOOSE MACHINES—A SCIENCE

ANNE D.

Anne is a 40-year-old mortgage broker from Long Island. She plays the slots both at the casinos in Atlantic City and in the casinos "in the woods" in Connecticut. She, like so many successful parlorites, went from being a loser to being a winner at the slots by learning to better distinguish the loose machines from the tight ones. We've already learned the basics of this practice, but Anne has turned the process into something of a science—and a lucrative science at that.

"When I first started playing slot machines, I played any old machine," Anne says. "Actually, that's not true. I played the machines that I thought looked good. I would play the ones with the brightest lights and the snazziest design— none of which had anything whatsoever to do with my luck. So naturally, I usually lost. Then I found out that winning at the slots was not merely a matter of luck. I found out that the machines are preset to be loose or tight, and the real trick was to figure out which was which. As was true of men as well, the first thing I had to do was get it out of my head that I would be able to tell the winning slot machines from the losers just by looking at them."

Here are Anne's rules for determining which machines in the casino are the loosest.

"Unless there are some real slot-machine-aholics in the casino, the only people there who are there regularly enough to know which machines pay out the most over the long haul are the employees. The managers of the casinos and the people who program the machines know the payback rates of each machine, too—but that doesn't do you any good, because they aren't going to tell you. The people who work at the casino, though—making change or serving drinks or whatever it is that they do—should have the best knowledge of all, if they're observant. So the first thing you do when you get to the slot parlor is find slot changers who look like maybe they haven't been rendered brain dead by the boredom of their job, and, along with a nifty tip, you ask them where the hot machines are.

"Sometimes that doesn't work. Sometimes you don't find anybody who seems to have been paying attention. You get a lot of: 'I just started working here yesterday.' Or the dreaded: 'They seem all about the same to me,'" Anne continues. "So the next thing you do is keep an eye out for machines that are hot at the moment. Forget about which machines have the best payback rate over the long haul for the time being and think about which machine is hot *right now*. If you see a machine that's making a player rich, steadily giving out more than it's taking, and that machine becomes available, do not walk, run to get on that machine. There is always a chance that someone else has had an eye on that machine as well, and you don't want to get beaten to the punch."

And what if such a situation doesn't develop—or if by happenstance you're in the casino when there aren't enough other players to determine which machines are running hot?

"Then," Anne explains, "you have to try and get inside the psychology of the casino. If I was a casino owner, and I was making the bulk of my income from the slot machines, where would I put the loose machines and where would I put the tight ones? You can't have too many loose machines or else you wouldn't make any money, and you can't have too many tight machines or the players will stop playing. There has to be a pattern.

"I guess just about everybody knows that there are hardly ever two loose machines directly next to each other in a bank of machines. That's because so many slots players play two machines at the same time, which are, out of necessity, directly next to each other. That way, a player lucky enough to get a loose machine is also playing the tight machine next to it, so the casino breaks even.

"I know that a lot of experts [including this one—M.S.] think that there are a disproportionate number of slot machines in areas of heavy traffic in the casino, the thinking being that, when players win, the most people will see and hear them and this will make more people play the slots at the casino. I believe that this may be true of big-jackpot machines, because it's really only the big-jackpot winners who make the kind of fuss that's going to attract customers. Most of the winners at slots are winning quietly. They're putting in four coins and getting back five, again and again. They aren't screaming and yelling with joy, and no alarms are going off. There's no reason to put these machines out in the open. Instead, they're usually put in the place where the long-term steady slots player likes to play the most. I know of no regular slots players who like to play with their back to a busy aisle, so I doubt that the casinos are putting too many loose machines there. Too far back in the corner in the dark isn't good either, because regular slots players like to keep an eye on their fellow players. Therefore, I think the loosest machines are just a little bit off the beaten path.

"There's also a common belief—and this one I believe to be true—that machines that face the table games are usually extremely tight. That's because the people who play at the tables usually frown upon slot machines, so no matter how many slots players are winning in their vicinity, they aren't going to switch games. There's no point in trying to impress them.

"If you follow these clues, you may not be able to walk up to a machine and say, 'This one is loose.' But by avoiding the areas where there are many tight machines, you greatly increase the chances that the machine you pick will be loose," concludes Anne.

CASE HISTORY XVI: PLAY ONE MACHINE AT A TIME

WILLIAM K.

William K. is a 67-year-old retired electrician from Darby, Pennsylvania, a suburb of Philadelphia. He went from being a loser to being a winner in the slots parlor simply by breaking one longtime habit.

"I was one of those fellows who always played two machines at the same time," William says. "I believed that by playing two machines at once I had twice as much of a chance of winning a big jackpot.

"I also thought that I was doubling my excitement. I had one set of reels moving at all times. So while I was inserting the coins and pulling the handle on one, the reels would be spinning on the other, and vice versa. I figured that I was maximizing the experience, and there may have been some truth to that. But what was *not* true was that I was helping my chances of winning. In fact, I have learned that by playing two adjacent machine at all times, I was playing right into the casino's hands.

"As I look back on it, the truth was so obvious that I'm a little bit embarrassed that I had to be told about it, that I never figured it out on my own. The casinos, you see, know how much people love to play two machines at once, so they always put cold machines right next to hot ones. That way, the money you're taking in on the machine on the right is being sucked right back by the machine on the left.

"I guess if you were in a relatively empty casino and you had very, very long arms so that you could play every other machine simultaneously, you might have a shot at leaving the place a winner, but as long as the two machines you're playing simultaneously are adjacent, you haven't got a chance of coming out on top.

"I stopped being a two-machine player altogether. I now concentrate my energies on identifying the hot machine. And when I find it, I play it for all it's worth.

"And you know what? Not only am I winning more and losing less, but I'm also having more fun. I guess I had mistaken playing slot machines with aerobic exercises or working on an assembly line or something. I was a constant motion machine, so that I never stopped to appreciate anything. Even when I was taking in coins, I was doing it as fast as I could so that I could get them into the machine that had fallen momentarily idle. It's not worth it."

That's the lesson here. Slow down and enjoy playing your slot machine. It's more fun, and the odds of winning are better as well.

CASE HISTORY XVII: DON'T GO BY BRAND NAMES

PAULINE P.

Pauline P. is a 51-year-old housewife from Portland, Oregon. Her quantum leap in slots profits came after she recognized a basic misconception she'd had regarding the looseness and tightness of various machines.

"I guess I've never been much for generic products," Pauline says. "I've always believed in brand names. People would tell me that the generic was 'just as good, only cheaper.' But I never believed it. I trusted the brand names that I heard on commercials on television. And I trusted the logos on the labels that I recognized and was familiar with.

"So I guess it's only logical that when I started to play the slots, I thought the same way. I tended to think that if I played a Bally's quarter machine with a picture of a pink flamingo on it, and it did well for me, all Bally's machines with pictures of pink flamingos on them were loose. So I'd seek out every machine just like that under the assumption that I had the system figured out and was going to make a mint.

"On the other hand, if I played a Golden Nugget Silver Dollar machine with a big cherry on it and it was tighter than a rusty lug nut, then I'd never, ever play a Golden Nugget Silver Dollar machine with a cherry on top again.

"I was the most surprised girl in the world when it was finally explained to me that the brand had nothing to do with it. The manufacturers of the machines did in fact determine the payback rates of the machines, but they did it according to the specifications of the casino honchos, who had to keep within legal limits.

"That meant that the pink flamingo slot in one casino could be tight while the exact same model of machine in another casino—or down the aisle a way in the same casino, for that matter—could be loose as a goose.

"Now I know that it does matter if it's a nickel machine or a silver dollar machine, and it does matter if it's Trump or Caesars, and it does matter if you're in the corner or on an aisle—but it doesn't matter who made the machine, and it doesn't matter what theme or design the machine has. Got it?"

CASE HISTORY XVIII: STICK WITH A WINNER

PATRICIA L.

Patricia L. is 26 years old and works in a copy shop in a small college town in New England.

"I never went to casinos much before I went to school in this town, and then decided to stay after I graduated. There are a couple of huge casinos in Connecticut, and I go to both of them regularly," she says.

"When I first started going, I used to have hot streaks a lot when I played the slot machines. But for reasons that I had yet to figure out, I used to hardly ever leave the slots parlor ahead of the game. What would happen is, I'd get on a hot machine and I'd be filling my cup with coins again and again. But instead of sticking with that machine and taking it for all it was worth, I'd become impatient. I'd become convinced that the machine was about to turn icy cold and that what I had to do was find another hot machine.

"Well, you can figure out what usually happened. I'd walk away from the hot machine, oblivious to the three players who fought for it the second I got off my stool, and I'd go on to a machine where I would systematically pump all of my winnings—plus a little more to boot—right back into the slot.

"Now, slot machines are a lot like the stock market. There is no telling when your luck has peaked and the tide is turning. So now I stick with the hot machine a lot longer than I used to. I make the hot machine turn cold before I get off. Usually if I play seven or eight times on a formerly hot machine and get bupkis in return, I know that it's time to move on.

"Experience has taught me that I lose less of my profits letting the hot machine take a little back than I did when I abandoned the hot machine and used my profits to try and warm up a second machine."

CASE HISTORY XIX: MANAGING STRESS

PAUL P.

Paul P. is a 43-year-old printer from upstate New York who says that managing his stress was the biggest hurdle he had to leap before he could become a slots player who won on a regular basis.

"I found that, in order to overcome the house advantage and take advantage of all of my advantages, I had to concentrate very hard. I was getting stressed out. Here I was, getting stressed out over playing slots, a pastime that, for many, produces an almost trancelike state of complete relaxation. But I knew that those people were paying a price for that relaxation, and I wasn't willing to do that. It got to be a real problem. I would come down with blinding headaches while playing the machines. The ringing and dinging that's usually music to my ears—because I love to play the slots, really I do—was like a horrible static that was burning pain into my brain. Naturally, when that happened, my ability to concentrate went out the window and all the strategies and techniques for winning that I had taught myself over the years flew right out the window—along with my bankroll. Then I discovered that it wasn't just the way I behaved in the casino that was causing my problem, it was my lifestyle, period. I took a course in managing my stress and I learned that my sleeping habits, diet, exercise, and the techniques I use to relax were all factors when it came to minimizing my stress.

"I read a book called *Good Food, Good Mood,* and it taught me how I could actually accentuate the positive attitude that it takes to win at slots through eating the right things. I learned that quickest mood swings are caused by a fluctuation in the amount of sugar in your bloodstream. Don't bring a bag full of Hershey Kisses with you when you're in a slots parlor. Not only are you apt to leave the handle sticky, but you're also going to give yourself a sugar rush—which might be pleasant enough, if not a little frantic—followed by an insulin rush, which is apt to leave you fidgety on your stool and maybe even smacking the machine a few times with a closed fist when it turns out to be too tight for you. Of course, it doesn't have to be just candy. All in all, I've found that it isn't a good idea to play immediately after eating a large meal. You're apt to be drowsy for a while, as your digestive processes are busy, and there was apt to have been a lot of sugar somewhere in the meal—not to mention the dessert.

"I've found that, if I plan on playing the slots for long hours—and that's the way I prefer to play—and I want to stay as alert as possible so that I can always maintain my strategy to the T, I eat four or five very small meals evenly spaced in time over the course of the day. I say 'evenly spaced' with a wink, because it's almost impossible to get out of the parlor on a regular basis, especially when things are going well. I'll be damned if I'm going to leave a machine just to catch a bite to eat. However, when that does happen, and my machines cool off as they always do, I won't stuff myself in order to make up for the meal I missed. And I never drink. Alcohol burns even faster than sugar. It's like trying to keep your internal fireplace going by feeding it nothing but balled-up newspaper. The four or five small meals amount to small logs, which keep that fire burning strong and steady throughout the day and night."

But even more so than a bad diet, sleeplessness or a constantly changing sleep pattern had an effect on Paul P.'s ability to execute his game plan while playing the slots.

"I learned that playing long hours deep into the night wasn't doing anything for my bank account. I was making mistakes late at night that I wouldn't have made hours earlier when I was feeling relatively refreshed. Now, even though I am in theory 'on vacation' when I'm in the casino, I still try to get to bed at a reasonable hour. And I don't allow myself to sleep in late in the morning, even though there are some mornings when that's very hard. I try to keep my hours as close to those of my work week as possible.

"And because I know that I'm a person who's crisp and clear thinking in the morning and in the evening—and just a tad lazy in the afternoon—I plan my break for the afternoon, when I know my skills are apt to be at their least sharp to begin with."

And what is Paul's favorite relaxation technique?

"I lie on my back in bed and one at a time I relax all of the parts of my body until, by the time all of my parts are relaxed, I feel as if I weigh about 500 pounds and am drifting around in space."

A few minutes of that, Paul says, and he's ready for another couple of hours of playing the slots!

APPENDIX
THE HISTORY OF
SLOT MACHINES

Since 1980 a piece of granite with a plaque affixed to it, sometimes known as California Historical Marker 937, has sat in San Francisco at the confluence of Battery, Market, and Bush streets.

The marker was placed there by the benevolent fraternity known as the Ancient and Honorable Order of *E Clampus Vitus,* which usually focuses its charitable activities upon the needs of widows and orphans.

But this marker had nothing to do with either. It was placed on its site to commemorate the invention of the slot machine—the first "one-armed bandit."

The story goes that the slot machine was invented in the 1890s by a Bavarian immigrant named Charles Fey. This San Franciscan mechanic has become known as the "Thomas Edison of Slot Machines."

Fey built a gambling device based on spinning wheels and matching symbols. There was a slot in which to deposit one coin, and a tray at the bottom where you plucked out your winnings if you lined up three symbols. And of course there was a handle, one, on the right.

The machine sat on bar tops in San Francisco saloons, and a winning spin earned the player a free drink. It wasn't long, however, before the machines offered greater stakes.

The plaque that marks the site now reads:

> The first slot machines were manufactured by the inventor Charles Fey just west of this site at 406 Market from 1896 till the factory was destroyed in the 1906 earthquake and fire. Fey dubbed his invention the "Liberty Bell" in honor of the famous symbol of freedom. Ultimately, the slot machine became the most famous gambling device of all time.

Fey liked building slot machines so much that it was pretty much all he did for the next 30 years.

There had been gambling devices before Fey's invention, however. The earliest machines, dating back well into the 19th century, were most often based on a wheel-of-fortune format, with a nickel turning into a quarter if the lucky number comes up. (Now, if there had been only a little mechanical Vanna White to flip over letters, they might have been on to something.)

In 1876 the McLoughlin Company manufactured a little machine called the "Guessing Bank" that was designed to sit on the counter at the cigar store. Whenever a customer bought a cigar, he would get a free play on the Guessing Bank. If the customer didn't buy a cigar, the Guessing Bank cost a nickel. Drop in the nickel and the wheel with numbers spun around. If the customer correctly guessed what number the wheel would stop at, he received a quarter. Many versions of this machine were available for cigar stores and saloons, but my favorite is the one that was built to look like a little Ferris wheel. It was called—get ready to groan—the "Fairest Wheel."

Charles Fey's first slot machines had three reels with 10 symbols on each reel, so that the odds against getting three of a kind were 1,000 to 1.

However, three of a kind, when it came up, paid only 100 to 1, guaranteeing a healthy profit to the house. The odds weren't posted in those days—The Law had to get involved before casinos started explaining things on the front of slot machines—and it was so much fun to play that no one bothered to do the math and figure out just what a bad bet it was.

The symbols on the reels were the four suits used in a deck of cards (hearts, diamonds, spades, and clubs) as well as bells, horseshoes, and stars.

Fey diversified with the turn of the century. He manufactured the first mechanized game that simulated the rules of poker in 1901. Here's how Fey's poker slot paid out:

Combination	Free Cigars
Royal flush	50
Straight flush	20
Four Aces	10
Four Kings	8
Four Queens	7
Four under Queens	5
Full house	4
Flush	3
Straight	3

Three Aces	3
Three Kings	3
Three Queens	2
Three under Queens	2
Two pairs Aces up	2
Under Aces	1
Two Aces	1

LIBERTY BELLS

Fey's first slot machines, Liberty Bells, were manufactured one at a time and were made of cast iron. They were made at an appropriate size for sitting atop the bar in a tavern. Fey didn't just sell his machines to saloons, however. He also collected commissions. The profits brought in by the machines were split 50-50 by Fey and the bar owners.

Fey's monopoly on the slot machine business didn't last long. Since the slot machine was, by definition, a gambling device, it could not be patented.

MILLS IMITATES AND INNOVATES

In 1906 a man by the name of Herbert Stephen Mills got hold of a Fey slot machine, opened it up, saw how it was built, and immediately started making his own. Though Mills never drove Fey out of business (Fey continued making his machines until the 1930s), Mills was the first slot machine manufacturer to go national.

Since he hadn't broken the law, Mills was unashamed of the derivative nature of his product and called it the Mills Liberty Bell. His products were not without innovation, however. It was Mills who first thought of putting a window in the front of the machine so that prospective players could see all the coins that were already inside the machine. Players, of course, didn't view the coins as the losses of previous players, but as a jackpot waiting to be paid out to the next player.

Also, with the Fey machine only one row of symbols was visible at a time as the reels spun around. Mills, however, decided to offer his game a bit of excitement derived from wheels of fortune. On the Mills machine three rows were visible—the winning row, plus the row above and below it. Now, if players lost, they could look through the window in the front of the machine and see how close they'd come to winning.

The Mills machines came with a cast-iron case engraved with the Liberty Bell, the Statue of Liberty, and a view of New York Harbor (on the side).

Another Mills innovation, if that's the right word, was to increase the number of symbols on each reel from 10 to 20 so that the number of possible combinations increased from 1,000 to 8,000.

NEW SYMBOLS

Mills also changed the symbols that Fey used. Fruits replaced playing card suits, so cherries, lemons, and plums began to appear for the first time. The fruit motif remains a popular one on slot machines today.

Perhaps Mills's most influential innovation, however, was the introduction of the concept of a jackpot—an ultimate prize that would keep players coming back again and again no matter how much they had lost.

Before long many manufacturers were making slot machines, among them Rock-Ola, Caille Brothers, Evans, Keeney, Southern Doll, Snyder, and Daval.

These new copies were often exactly that: precise duplicates of Fey or Mills machines, right up to the designs on the cast-iron casing.

Caille was an exception. This company was trying something new. In 1907 Caille made the first double slot machine: two machines attached at the side. The one on the left took dimes, and the one on the right took quarters. It was called the Twin Centaur and weighed 440 pounds. Selling for a whopping $375, it's safe to say that none of these showed up in the back room of the neighborhood corner cigar store.

GUM AND CANDY MACHINES

Many of the antigambling laws currently on the books were first put into place around 1910 when there was a government crackdown on gambling. To stay in business, the manufacturers of slot machines had to be tricky.

Since slot machines that took coins and paid off in coins were now illegal in most places, manufacturers created machines that could be used for gambling purposes but were technically legal.

To do this, machines were made to pay off in gum or cheap candy. According to the law, these were now vending machines, and therefore quite legal.

The machine gave you a piece of gum for every coin you inserted. It was a vending machine, not a gambling device. However, if you got three bells or three cherries or whatever, it might pay off with 20 pieces of gum. Taverns, in this way, continued to use the machines as gambling devices. When a player won the extra gum or candy, he merely traded it in with the bartender for cash.

Another attempt to get around the gambling laws was to have machines pay off in coupons that could be exchanged for merchandise in whatever store the machine lived in. On these machines, if you won, you received a ticket that said it was good for 50 cents' worth of "trade" or merchandise. Whether the stores were actually paying off in "trade" or were converting that trade into cash for their gambling customers was a matter very difficult for the authorities to investigate.

PROHIBITION

The scam lasted until Prohibition. That was a period during the 1920s and early 1930s when all alcoholic beverages were illegal in the United States. Prohibition created more criminals than any other law in history.

Legal taverns were replaced with "speakeasies," illegal drinking establishments that had to keep themselves hidden from the cops. You needed to know the password to get inside, and once you were in, there were usually plenty of slot machines to play.

Since these were hidden from the authorities anyway, there was no reason to pretend that they were anything other than what they were. Slot machines again began to pay off in coins.

Since the machines themselves were hidden away, the police now turned their attention for the first time to stopping the manufacturing of slot machines. In 1933 police and press swooped down upon the plant of Charles Fey, seizing 200 slot machines.

In 1934, when Prohibition was repealed, booze was allowed to come out of the closet. Unfortunately, the slot machines that had lived inside those secret watering holes had to remain hidden. They were still illegal.

In New York City Mayor La Guardia posed for the newspapers in front of a mountain of slot machines, a sledge hammer in his hand. The machines were loaded onto barges and taken out to sea, where they were dumped, destined to live for all eternity in Davey Jones's locker.

BIRTH OF BALLY'S

Bally Manufacturing, which would become the top maker of slot machines in the world along with operating its own casinos in Las Vegas and Atlantic City, was formed in 1931. The company's first product was a penny pinball machine called the Ballyhoo.

Bally did make one interesting slot machine during its early days, but the company didn't become a major player in slot machine manufacturing until the 1960s. That early machine had one set of three reels and one handle on the right, but there were slots for coins on either side, nickels on the right and quarters on the left.

The same machine was available with nickel slots on either side and quarter slots on either side. The player had the option of playing either side one at a time or both sides at the same time.

THE NAKED LADY

In 1925 the Caille Company put out a revolutionary machine. Because a scantily clad woman who danced in the wind, her scarves blowing, was stamped in tin on the front of each machine, the model was known as "the Naked Lady."

Next to the Naked Lady was a button that automatically spun the wheels. There was also a "skill button," a regular hoax in those days, on the front. Around this button—which was placed directly to the left of the naked lady—it said, ARE YOU SKILFUL [sic]? PUSH BUTTON. CATCH A WINNER.

But it was not the risqué nature of its external design that made this machine revolutionary, but rather a mechanism on its inside. It was the first slot machine to have a "multiple coin slug detector," so that it was impossible to use it unless you inserted real quarters.

FOUR REELS AND OTHER LOSERS

Some of Caille's innovations caught on better than others. One item that's common now but was not well received when it was introduced is the fourth reel. At about that same time that the Naked Lady was first unveiled, the Caille Company also put out the first slot machine with four reels.

Players then as now could see that the fourth reel was going to do nothing to improve their chances of lining up fruit. The initial reaction to the four reels was complete rebellion and boycott. The machines simply went unused until many establishments were forced to cover the first reel and then pay out jackpots by hand when the machine had three of a kind on reels two through four.

Caille also tried a machine that had the handle in the middle. It was unpopular because of its uncanny resemblance to an aroused male. Many players felt uncomfortable yanking on such a handle.

THE GOLDEN AGE OF SILVER DOLLARS

Charles Fey made his last great contribution to slots in the last year of the Roaring Twenties. The thing that made the Twenties roar was the fact that a lot of people had a lot of money. This meant a lot of gambling, so it was a very good time for the slot machine biz. Little did these madcaps know that it was all about to go sour with the Wall Street crash and the Great Depression that followed.

It was into the wild, wild world of early 1929 that Fey introduced the great Silver Dollar Three-Reel Slot. Now, even in pre-depression America, a silver dollar was a lot of money to risk on a pull of the arm. For this reason, the machine became known as the Big Spender.

After the depression had passed, and World War II followed it, prosperity returned to the United States in the 1950s. Once again slot machines became popular—and among the most popular of all were the silver dollar slots.

It wasn't until the mints stopped making silver dollars, mostly because silver became too valuable, that people began to keep their silver dollars when playing the slots rather than cashing them in for paper money. Unable to constantly replenish the supply of silver dollars, since no new ones were being produced, the casinos were forced to stop using the silver dollar machines.

Now that there are again dollar coins being made—this time gold in color with the Native American woman Sacagawea on them—perhaps one day dollar machines that accept dollar coins will be available. But this isn't going to happen until casinos are confident that the dollar coins currently being minted will have some longevity. Attempts to replace the silver dollar in the past have been short lived, so until the current coin proves to have some shelf life, slot machines are going to continue insisting upon paper money or quarters.

The Fey family is still very involved in the slot machine business. Marshall and Frank Fey, the sons of Charles, own and operate a saloon/restaurant/museum in Reno, Nevada, known as The Liberty Belle. It boasts the nation's largest collection of vintage slot machines. Besides slots there are arcade machines, a beautiful Brunswick "Del Monico" back bar, two immense combination gas and electric brass chandeliers, original leaded-glass shades, numerous beer trays, a multitude of early advertisements, firearms, old photographs, Edison phonographs, and huge brass cash registers. The museum has as its featured attractions the first three-reel slot machine, the first Draw Poker machine, and the first Silver Dollar Three-Reel Slot.

GAMBLING SHIPS

During the years before the start of World War II, one of the ways that people gambled legally in the United States was to board a ship, which would then sail more than three miles offshore into international waters. Outside the legal

U.S., these ships were then immune from U.S. laws, which meant that gambling was legal.

The most famous of these gambling ships was the SS *Rex,* which could hold almost 2,000 gamblers. It floated outside American waters off the coast of California and was a favorite for gamblers from the Southern California region. It has been estimated that almost a million people visited the ship during its years of operation. There were 65 gaming tables and 120 slot machines aboard. Though the ships were, in theory, operating legally, not all officials agreed, or cared.

In 1939 Attorney General Earl Warren, who would later become the chief justice of the U.S. Supreme Court, ordered the ships raided and the equipment seized.

Earl Warren, who fancied himself a "crime buster" like Eliot Ness, did not give up on his war against slot machines. In 1950 Warren—by this time the governor of California— signed the "$500 Possession" law, which stated that any establishment caught in possession of a slot machine would be fined $500—per machine! Slowly, Southern Californians came to grips with the reality—inconvenient but not impossible to deal with—that they were going to have to cross the border into Nevada if they wanted to play the slots.

SLOTS GO TO WAR

When World War II came to America with the attack on Pearl Harbor by the Japanese on December 7, 1941, the top manufacturers of slot machines at the time all stopped making machines of chance and instead converted their facilities to the production of war matériel.

The Mills Company performed more than 40 different jobs for the War Department, building tail fins for airplanes, turret assemblies for battle tanks, as well as parts for bombs. When the war ended in 1945, manufacturers had just gotten back into the swing of making slot machines again when, in 1951, the U.S. Congress passed the Johnson Act, which took the law in California and pretty much applied it nationwide.

Companies tried to find new clients in Europe as quickly as they could, but the sudden reduction in the number of possible customers caused hard times and, in many cases, shutdowns in operations.

WOODEN INDIANS

During the late 1940s and early 1950s a sculptor named Frank Polk carved and painted almost 100 life-sized wooden Indians, leaving a hole in the chest and belly for a slot machine. Machines manufactured by both Pace and Mills fit.

Polk didn't just carve Indians, however; there were cowboys with slot machines in their bellies as well. The figures became a beloved part of Nevada culture—so much so that for the last 30 years, other artists have been commissioned by casinos to carve similar life-sized cowboys and Indians. Polk's originals have taken on a nostalgic aura in Las Vegas—like the thought of a Rat Pack reunion. Or the days when Elvis imitators weren't necessary, because Vegas still had the real King.

THE RISE AND FALL AND RISE OF MILLS

The Mills Company had grown huge by the 1940s. Its three factories in Chicago employed more than 3,000 people. Then came slower times. By the 1950s two of the Mills brothers had passed away. The call for new slot machines was light at this time; the company had been surviving by making Coca-Cola machines.

Mills made beautiful machines. Along with slots and Coke machines, it was known for art deco jukeboxes and guess-your-weight scales. But then Mills lost its Coke contract, and the company folded. Only its slot division survived, sold and moved to Reno. Innovations came forthwith.

O. D. JENNINGS

When the war was over, O. D. Jennings replaced Mills as the company putting out the most innovative slot machines. The new machines were luxurious stand-up models, cased in wood, with footrests in case you were in front of them while sitting on a bar stool.

These were the first slot machines to come with their own lights—to make it easier to read the award card. The model known as the "Sweepstakes Console," which made its debut in 1950, had a holder for the player's coin cup.

The Jennings machines often had an Indian theme to their design. Another Jennings innovation of the period was the crisscross machine, which showed three lines of symbols on each reel and played tic-tac-toe.

THE FIRST BAR MACHINE

In 1954 Mills manufactured the first bar machine, known as the Roto-Slot machine. Meant to be played from above, the slot was set into a cocktail table so that players could relax in a lounge and have a drink while playing their own personal slot. The reels were viewed through a glass window in the table. There was a slot for the coin; the only thing that stuck out of the table surface was the handle. The machine first appeared at the Sands Hotel in Las Vegas.

DOUBLE SLOTS

In the early 1960s some clever casino operator discovered that the state of Nevada was taxing slot machines by the handle rather than by the slot. To exploit this law, the Mills Company was commissioned to build double-slot machines. Two slot machines with two separate and independently working sets of reels—but only one handle.

Players could play two machines simultaneously while pulling the handle only once. (Knowing what we know, you can bet that one side was loose and the other tight. One giveth and one taketh away.)

BALLY, HI!

One of the biggest leaps in slot machine technology came in 1963. Illinois, up until this time, had banned the manufacturing of gambling devices. But the law was repealed in 1963, so Bally Manufacturing of Chicago was able to make slot machines.

It turned out that Bally was, by far, better at making the machines than anyone had been before. It gave its machines "electro-mechanical circuitry." Now slots could take one, two, or three coins and pay off in multiples, so that the more you played, the more you won. The new machine's payout unit could dish out varying amounts, allowing a multitude of winning combinations—some, of course, better than others.

The first modern Bally slot was called the "Money Honey," and it was without a doubt rookie of the year in Las Vegas for 1964. The next Bally innovation came in 1967 when the more dryly named "Five-Coin Multiplier" was introduced, taking up to five coins per play.

In the 30 years since, slot machines—like everything else, it seems—have become computerized, but the bulk of slot machines in most casinos remain mechanical. People, as it turns out, appreciate the fact that those reels are really spinning.

Where they stop, nobody knows.

GLOSSARY

Attract mode   When a slot machine is idle, the machine will often play music or flash colorful lights to attract players to it.

Autobet   Some newfangled machines, which operate on credit rather than coins, allow players to repeat the same bet again and again by pressing a button.

Bank   A row of slots.

Banner   A message in lights that crawls across a machine, usually a computerized machine, designed to attract or inform a player.

Bar machine   A machine designed to sit atop a bar or counter. Usually you look down into spinning symbols, so the machine appears to be on its back rather than upright. Also known as a flat top.

Belly glass   The lower glass on the door of a machine through which you can read the pay table, the denomination of the table, or the theme of the game. The belly glass is the most frequently broken part of a slot machine, usually cracked by a player who, perhaps in a bad mood, has struck it with a fist.

Big Bertha   The biggest slot machine in the casino. It's usually placed close to the casino's entrance or at the beginning of the slot machine section. It's designed to attract attention, with bells and whistles galore, and has a huge handle and 10 reels.

Bill acceptor   A slot through which a player slides paper money in return for change or credit. Many modern slot machines now have their own bill-accepting change machine.

Blank   A stopping position on a reel upon which there is no symbol. Sometimes jackpot-only machines have many blanks. Machines with many blanks are known to be tight, so lay off.

Buy-a-pay   A machine whose pay table changes depending on the number of coins you play. On these machines the jackpot is almost always available only to those who wager the maximum number of coins. These machines are sometimes known by the symbol that wins the jackpot if the maximum wager is played, such as a "Buy the Bars" machine.

Cabinet   The outer shell of a slot machine, sometimes made of laminated wood, usually covering a metallic interior.

Carousel Sometimes casinos arrange their slot machines in a circle. In the middle, in a high chair, sits the person who makes change. Carousels are becoming less and less frequent now that modern slot machines come with their own automatic change makers.

Cash-out switch A switch on some machines that can convert credit into cash or cashable vouchers.

Change person An employee of the casino who breaks paper money into coin change for slot machine players. These people are slowly but surely being replaced by automatic change makers built right into the slot machines.

Coin comparitor A mechanism within a slot machine that checks the coin you've just inserted and verifies that is a real coin of the desired denomination. The mechanism uses a sample coin to check against each coin inserted. If the coins don't match, your coin will be rejected by the machine.

Coin in A meter inside the slot machine that counts the number of coins that have been inserted. In modern machines, usually computerized, the coin in and the coin comparitor have been merged into a single apparatus that counts, verifies, and routes the coins. Naturally, since there's a coin in, there's also a . . .

Coin out A meter inside the machine that counts the number of coins the machine has paid out. The coin in and coin out are included in the software of computerized machines.

Coin tray The metal tray upon which the payout coins fall and can be retrieved by the player.

Credit   As in "one credit": the value equivalent to one coin in the denomination that the machine uses. In a quarter machine that takes credit, a dollar bill will get you four credits. Get a card from the casino to plug in and be billed later if you play more than you win.

Credit limit   The maximum number of credits that can be counted in a machine before a player must either put money into the machine (if she's losing) or cash out (if she's winning).

Credit mode   A machine ready to accept paper money and give credits is in credit mode.

Drop   The amount of money in the drop box, usually thought of in terms of money played minus money paid out.

Drop box   The container in which played money accumulates after it spills out of the full hopper.

Fill   When a machine runs out of coins, an employee of the casino comes with a big bag and refills the machine—that is, he pours the coins into the machine's hopper.

Flat top   *See* Bar machine.

Fruit reel machine   A favorite. This is a slot machine that features different kinds of fruits on the reels. Fruit reel machines usually don't have blanks. The nonfruit symbols on fruit reel machines are usually 7s.

Handle pulls   The total number of plays. This is different from the money taken in on machines in which different numbers of coins may be played on each pull.

Handle slammers Cheaters. Years ago, before computerization and high-tech construction, it was possible to make a slot machine pay off by manipulating the handle in a certain manner. People who cheated in this manner were called handle slammers.

Hand pay Some machines don't hold the cash for their own jackpot. Rather, when you win the jackpot on that machine, the usual racket ensues and an attendant brings you your money.

Hit frequency Assuming that all combinations of symbols are equally likely to appear, the hit frequency is the ratio of winning combinations to the total number of possible combinations. This should, in theory, be equal to the ratio of actual winning plays to plays.

Hold The percentage of coins that a machine takes in and never pays back out. In other words, the hold is the profit that the casino makes. The hold on slot machines is anywhere from 3 percent up to 15 percent—although there are certainly machines out there with a hold larger than that. You calculate the hold by subtracting the payback percentage from 100 percent.

Hopper The assembly inside the machine where the coins are stored. When a machine's hopper becomes filled to overflowing, the excess coins discreetly drop into a bucket below called the drop box. These buckets are emptied quietly once a day. Casinos, of course, do not want to make a big deal about machines becoming too full. When a machine becomes empty, there is a whole production while more coins are put in. Emptying the hopper is done much more discreetly.

Idle mode   *See* Attract mode.

Jackpot   Any slot machine's largest payout. Most machines have smaller payouts as well, little mood boosters to keep you playing.

Jackpot-only machine   A slot machine that doesn't have smaller payouts, as most machines do. Either you win the jackpot or you don't get your coin back.

Liberty Bell   The name of the first slot machine, invented in the 19th century in San Francisco by Charles Fey.

Lineup   A game in which symbols must line up for a player to win. In the 21st century this term refers both to machines that have actual spinning reels with symbols on them and to computerized games that simulate spinning wheels on a screen.

Loose machine   A slot machine that pays off more frequently than others.

Low-level machines   Slots designed to be played while sitting down. Almost all varieties of slots come in a low-level model.

Maximum bet   The maximum number of coins a player can put into a machine for one play. It's almost always the maximum bet that makes a player eligible for the maximum jackpot. On some machines you can play anywhere from one to six coins on each pull of the handle, but on most machines the maximum bet is less than six.

Mills machines The brand name of the first slot machines to be used in the United States coast to coast. They were the first machines to feature the concept of a jackpot, and the first to use fruit on their reels.

One-armed bandit A slot machine. The term comes from a court case during the 1930s. A judge, when sentencing a man for illegally operating a gambling device, said, "The machine is a one-armed bandit!" The name stuck.

Overlay A symbol that has been pasted onto a reel over another symbol, the result almost always being that the machine now has fewer winning combinations. If you're in a casino and you see that its machines have overlays, move on. Most casinos these days don't feel it necessary to make their machines any tighter after they're in place. They're doing just fine the way things are. You're most apt to see an overlay on a machine in the bus station in Lovelock, Nevada, or something like that. Once again, my advice is, move on.

Partial pay Everyone loves the mad rush of coins belching out of a slot machine when they have just hit the jackpot. But there are times when the jackpot is so large that paying off in this manner would be impractical. If you were to hit a million-dollar jackpot on a silver dollar machine, the ensuing pile of coins would be higher than the ceiling. In some cases there are merely bells and whistles from the machine; a casino attendant comes to you with the remainder of your cash. Then there's partial pay, which is actually the solution that's the most fun and practical. In this system, when you hit the jackpot, you still get the joy of the coins rushing out into your eager fingers. But only part of the jackpot comes this way. An attendant soon comes by with the remainder of your booty in a more practical paper form.

Payback percentage   The number of coins a player wins divided by the number of coins she has played computed over a long period of time.

Pay cycle   A slot machine is in its pay cycle when, after taking in a certain number of coins, it must pay out in order to meet the percentage of payout programmed into its software.

Payline   The line of symbols, usually in the middle of the window in the front of the slot machine, in which matches pay off. Some machines have three or five paylines.

Payout   Your winnings from a single play.

Pay table   The mathematical equation by which a machine knows when to pay off. It's a chart of pay amounts as a function of each winning combination and, when applicable, the number of coins bet.

Percentage hold   *See* Hold.

Printed ticket   Some machines don't pay off in cash when you win the jackpot. Instead they dispense a printed ticket, which you then take to a casino attendant to be redeemed for cash.

Prize amount   Another way to say "size of the jackpot." The prize amount stays the same on some machines and changes on others depending on how long it has been since the jackpot was last won (progressive machines).

Progressive machines   Machines that don't have a preset amount for their jackpots, but rather have a jackpot that starts small and grows depending on how many coins have been played since the last jackpot was paid out.

Reels   These are the wheels with symbols on the outside that spin inside the slot machine. There are usually three reels. If all three reels stop with cherries on the payline, expect a pay-off. Some slot machines have more than three reels, and on these it is exponentially more difficult to hit a jackpot.

Reel strip   The strip with the symbols printed on it that's attached to the outer edge of the reel.

Runaway   A machine that empties as if a jackpot has just been won even though a jackpot has not been won. This is a heartbreaker, and luckily it doesn't occur very frequently. If it happens to you, however, remember that the money is not legally yours. If you try to grab the coins and make a run for it, you'll be charged with stealing. Instead, wait for the casino employees to come to the machine. They will give you whatever your payout was supposed to be and put the rest of the coins back into the hopper. (More likely, they will shut down the machine for repairs.)

Short drop   A machine malfunction. If you just got, say, two lemons and the machine is supposed to pay you six coins but in fact pays you only five, it's called a short drop. If this happens to you, contact a casino employee before you play again, and the difference will be made good to you.

Slot mix   The positioning of slot machines by casino executives to maximize earnings. Tight and loose machines are placed in particular areas and in a particular order to generate the maximum income while giving the impression that the machines are generous.

Spin button   When playing slot machines for many hours on end, some players grow weary of pulling the long handle mounted on the right side. Therefore, most modern slots come with a button. Put your coin in, push the button, and the reels spin just as if you had pulled the handle.

Stand-up machines   Slots designed to be played while standing up.

Steaming   Playing one machine for a long period of time in the hope of winning a big jackpot.

Straight slots   Machines with payouts whose amounts are set in stone. A progressive machine is not a straight machine. Usually the payout numbers are written right on the front of a straight machine.

Symbols   The images on the outsides of the reels that spin around when you pull the slot machine's arm. When the machine's reels stop with the same symbol on the payline, there is a payoff.

Take cycle   The exact opposite of the pay cycle. This is a period in which the machine must take in more coins that it pays out in order to meet its preprogrammed payout percentage.

Tight machine   A slot machine that pays off less frequently than others.

Tilt   The term comes from pinball machines. From Soho down to Brighton, when an overzealous pinball player would tilt the machine in an illegal attempt to alter the course of the silver ball, the machine would turn off and the player would lose his game. Likewise, when a slot machine turns off and won't function, it's called a tilt, even though no one has tilted the machine. When it comes to slots, a tilt usually occurs when a coin has become jammed inside or the machine has run out of coins.

Toke   A tip or gratuity, such as you might give a casino employee who points out a loose machine.

Well   The metal area at the bottom of a slot machine where payout coins drop. It's from the well that players collect their winnings.

Window   The glass in the front of a slot machine through which you see the spinning reels.

SUGGESTED READING

Allen, J. Edward. *The Basics of Winning Slots,* 3rd ed. New York: Cardoza Publishing, 2000.

Anderson, Ian. *Turning the Tables on Las Vegas.* New York: The Vanguard Press, 1976.

Cardoza, Avery. *Secrets of Winning Slots: Learn How to Beat the Casino at Slots!* New York: Cardoza Publishing, 1998.

Fey, Marshall. *Slot Machines: A Pictorial History of the First 100 Years,* 5th ed. Reno, Nev.: Liberty Belle Books, 1997.

Halcombe, Claude. *Slot Smarts: Winning Strategies at the Slot Machine.* New York: Carol Publishing Group, 1997.

Korfman, Tony. *Slots: Playing to Win.* Las Vegas, Nev.: Gaming Books International, 1985.

Regan, Jim. *Winning at Slot Machines.* Secaucus, N.J.: Citadel Press, 1998.

ABOUT THE AUTHOR

MacIntyre Symms has, under a variety of names, made a living in the following fields: social research, adult entertainment, and photography. Sometimes they overlapped. But his true love is the casino. Symms is single and currently lives in New York City.